ADVERTISING REACH AND FREQUENCY

COLIN MCDONALD

ADVERTISING REACH AND FREQUENCY

Maximizing Advertising Results Through Effective Frequency

SECOND EDITION

First Edition by Michael J. Naples

Published in conjunction with the Association of National Advertisers by NTC Business Books

Printed on recyclable paper

Association of National Advertisers, Inc.

NTC Business Books
a division of *NTC Publishing Group* • Lincolnwood, Illinois USA

Library of Congress Cataloging-in-Publication Data

McDonald, Colin.
    Advertising reach and frequency : maximizing advertising results
through effective frequency / Colin McDonald. — 2nd ed.
       p.   cm.
    Includes bibliographical references and index.
    ISBN 0–8442–3506–7 (hard)
    1. Advertising—Effective frequency. I. Title
HF5827.M19   1995
659.1—dc20   95–18555
                                               CIP

Published in conjunction with the Association of National Advertisers, Inc.
by NTC Business Books, 4255 West Touhy Avenue, Lincolnwood (Chicago),
Illinois 60646–1975, U.S.A.

CONTENTS

ABOUT THE ASSOCIATION OF NATIONAL ADVERTISERS

The Association's offices are located at:

155 East 44th St.
New York, New York 10017-4270
Telephone: 212-697-5500
Facsimile: 212-661-8057

700 11th St.
Suite 650
Washington DC 20001
Telephone: 202-626-7800
Facsimile: 202-626-6161

The Association of National Advertisers, Inc. (A.N.A.) is the industry's oldest trade association and the only organization exclusively dedicated to serving the interests of corporations that advertise regionally and nationally. The Association's membership is a cross-section of American industry, consisting of manufacturers, retailers, service providers, and financial institutions. Representing more than 5,300 separate advertising entities, these member companies market their products to consumers and to other companies. A.N.A. represents the needs of its members through advertising industry leadership, legislative leadership, information resources, professional development, and industry-wide networking.

Mission

To be broadly recognized as a highly innovative and aggressive association representing the leaders in American industry.

We will lead, not follow the industry, in meeting the needs of advertisers, agencies and the media.

We will act as a catalyst in bringing together industry leaders, advertising, marketing and communication professionals and members of other trade associations to confront pressing issues and explore emerging ideas critical to our industry.

FOREWORD

Publication of the original edition of *Effective Frequency* in 1979 was the culmination of a great deal of industry exploratory research, discussion, and debate on the subject together with the new availability of research studies specifically designed and carried out to probe the relationship between frequency of exposure to advertising and consumer response.

In his foreword to the original edition, Herbert E. Krugman succinctly summarized both the demand the book sought to fulfill as well as its intended contribution.

> The need for a current review of what is known about frequency springs in part from an escalation of media costs in recent years, especially in television, and the increased concern among advertisers not to spend more than is necessary and/or sufficient. Although precise levels of sufficiency require individual research on individual brands and markets, general guidelines and examples do emerge from the information presented in this book.

The book summarized the then-existing body of knowledge about effective frequency, including relevant proprietary studies which had been released to the Association of National Advertisers Research Policy Committee in order to round out the evidence brought to bear on this important media subject. Its publication substantially affected how media planners scheduled not only television, but radio and print as well. Yet, in doing so, many planners tended to oversimplify the application of general guidelines and conclusions into a 3-plus rule-of-thumb, which in turn legitimately led to a growth of criticism and debate about the concept of effective frequency.

It had been my hope in 1979 that we were on the leading edge of a new age of relevant data availability, both from the universal product code scanner as well as single-source data laboratories, which would lead to increased research on individual brands with regard to reach and frequency—and indeed from time to time over the past 16 years such research has been undertaken. Moreover, several ground-breaking print studies have been conducted, and in general the subject has become one of growing academic interest, bringing with it examination and constructive debate.

Given all that has gone before, together with more recent information and renewed interest in the concept, now seemed an appropriate time to revise the original edition. Moreover, the media itself has changed dramatically in recent years. Today's media world is one of high cable, vcr, and remote control penetration, greater broadcast and print fragmentation, and the emerging interactive era. The result is that there is, if anything, more interest today in the concept of effective frequency and its potential value for efficient media placement than ever before.

To update our knowledge on the subject I suggested that Colin McDonald, the noted British researcher and advertising analysis pioneer, undertake an updated edition incorporating all relevant information and debate on the concept since 1979. As you will see, as you become absorbed in the text of *Advertising Reach and Frequency: Maximizing Advertising Results Through Effective Frequency,* he has admirably summarized a great deal of new information and brought a much clearer perspective and a sharper degree of understanding of the underlying assumptions regarding effective frequency and how we as practitioners should view this information today.

While the subject of advertising frequency is no less difficult and challenging today, I am confident that Colin McDonald's incisive examination set forth here will provide a constructive basis for genuine progress.

Michael J. Naples
President
Advertising Research Foundation

ADVERTISING REACH AND FREQUENCY

CHAPTER 1

THE IMPORTANCE OF EFFECTIVE FREQUENCY

The term *effective frequency* refers to the range of exposures which are regarded as desirable for advertising to be effective. The underlying concept is that, if there is too little exposure, the advertising will fail to be noticed; on the other hand, if there is too much, the recipient will be "saturated" and the surplus will be redundant. At both extremes, the advertising expenditure will have failed to deliver value: it is therefore important for successful media planning to identify and seek to achieve the desired effective range.

The above definition is basic, oversimple, and begs a large number of practical questions. It describes merely the concept, without any indication of how in real life one might recognize the boundaries of "too little," "effective," or "too much." I will try to address these practical problems during the course of this book. Merely to state the concept, however, is enough to underline how important it is in times of ever-increasing pressure to squeeze the most value out of advertising spending.

MEDIA COST ESCALATION

The first edition of this book was published in 1979 by the Association of National Advertisers in response to a high level of expressed concern among the U.S. advertising community. For example, between June and August 1977, a mail survey was conducted by the newly-formed Media

1

Communications Council of the Advertising Research Foundation among 58 of the largest advertisers and 28 of the largest advertising agencies in the country. It was found that most respondents wanted to know more about the effects of one or more messages in terms of realized sales potential.

It was clear in 1979 that a major reason for the heightened interest in the subject of effective frequency was *the influence of media cost escalation* during the late 1970s, especially in television. This trend has continued. In Figure 1.1, updated figures are shown covering the entire period from 1960 to 1991 and projected through to 1993 for different media. Clearly, the cost escalation was greater during the 1980s than in previous years and, although the rate has slowed during the recessionary 1990s, it is rising.

The following discussion briefly covers what has been happening to the main media since 1979.

Television

The 1979 edition showed that costs per thousand in television rose steadily during the early 1970s until the 1974–75 season produced cost increases that once would have been considered intolerable. By this time, however, the advertising impact of television was so compelling and competitive activity so high, that advertisers had little choice but to pay. Nevertheless, the situation produced a new awareness of the need for efficient media scheduling, especially for smaller brands that can afford fewer and fewer messages. By 1979, television was consuming almost 60 percent of all national advertising dollars.

A number of problems were already becoming clear at that time. For example, while costs for prime time spots had more than doubled since 1970, the number of people reached by the average commercial in the same period went up by only 30 percent. As Fajen had put it in 1978:

> Obviously, the number of people reached has been outpaced by rising costs. In television, the basic yardstick for negotiation is cost per thousand (the amount it costs to reach 1,000 homes). Even this unit, which measures both costs and presumed value (homes reached), has increased 61 percent since 1970. Therefore, unless the viewer's ability to remember commercials has increased at that rate, today's dollar buys less in TV than yesterday's did.[1]

FIGURE 1.1A   Media Unit Cost Indexes

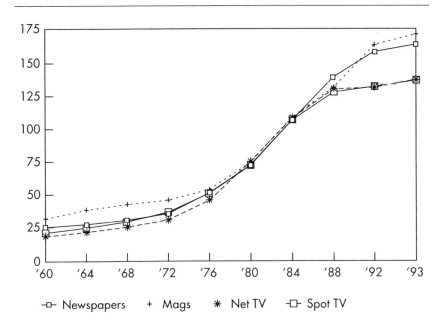

-□- Newspapers   + Mags   * Net TV   -□- Spot TV

FIGURE 1.1B   Media Unit Cost Indexes

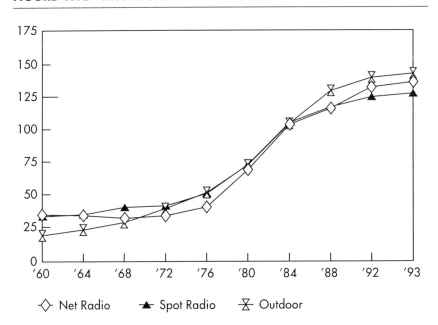

◇ Net Radio   ▲ Spot Radio   ✕ Outdoor

Source: McCann Erickson and *Advertising Age.*

Since the first edition, during the 1980s and early 1990s, television has not only continued to become more expensive, but the environment in which it operates has become steadily more complex and fragmented. Advertisers have many more options to reach consumers, but also more challenges and questions about how best to do so. During the 1980s, costs per thousand doubled in most dayparts for both network and spot television[2]; at the same time, the increasing difficulty of reaching viewers effectively further eroded the advertiser's ability to cover prospects effectively.

The increasing complexity of the television environment is illustrated by the following examples:

- The average number of channels receivable in U.S. homes with television increased from 10 in 1980 to 35 in 1992.[3]
- Average household viewing hours per week have increased from less than 47 at the end of the 1970s to 51 in 1992.[4] However, this increase in time spent watching television is not nearly large enough to offset the erosion of the major broadcast network ratings as a result of the proliferation of new channels and program sources. For example, the average three network prime time household rating has decreased from 16.0 in 1981 to 11.7 in 1992.[5]
- The increase in options for television during the 1980s is the result of:
  — Cable TV growth. Penetration of U.S. homes grew from 28 percent to 65 percent of all U.S. households between 1980 and 1992.[6]
  — Cable networks increased from a handful in the early 1980s to about 70 national and regional networks in 1992.[7]
  — The Fox network, a new broadcast entry in 1985, has been successful. Its ratings for some programs now equal or surpass those of the older broadcast networks.
- During the same period, independent programming increased significantly, further cutting into network ratings. The number of independent stations increased over 300 percent (to 430) during the 1980s.[8] Barter syndications, a major source of independent programming, became a large business, expanding from sales of $25 million in 1980 to $1.4 billion in 1992.[9] During the same period of time, total three network ad sales increased only 75 percent.

Another problem noted in 1979, which was already complicating the advertiser's task of effectively reaching target consumers, was *increasing clutter*. Originally, television had followed the radio convention of a 60-second commercial as the norm. By 1979, however, almost 90 percent of the commercials on television were 30-seconds rather than 60. During the 1980s, the 15-second commercial appeared, and by 1993 it accounted for a third of all commercials. In addition to shorter commercials, the networks have tended to increase the time they occupy. By 1979, more non-program announcements were being added by the networks, along with an additional minute of commercial time to movies and specials, and 10 seconds to newsbreak formats. Similar trends continued through the 1980s. Overall network clutter (the total number of announcements) is estimated to have increased more than 50 percent in the last 10 years.[10]

Increasing clutter inevitably has an important bearing on the effective frequency of television advertising since it becomes harder to make an impact through the medium. The Newspaper Advertising Bureau has reported that in the 1960s 34 percent of all viewers could name one or more products they had just seen advertised on TV, but by 1990 only 8 percent of viewers could do so.[11]

Another complicating factor has been the increased penetration of videotape recorders (VTRs), later videocassette recorders (VCRs). By 1979, VTRs were in about a million homes. By 1992, 79 percent of all households had VCRs and 81 percent had remote controls, giving the viewer greater potential for switching channels and zapping out commercials.[12] Total television now accounts for 56 percent of all national measured media expenditures. Cable and syndicated TV account for 8 percent of all expenditures.[13]

Radio

Radio's image is that of a more selective medium, something to be used on a local basis to round out advertising coverage—in many cases as a supplement to television's national reach. Radio has been the biggest loser to television, going from about a one-third share of advertiser expenditures before World War II to less than 10 percent in 1979 and 4.5 percent (of national measured media) in 1992. However, radio continues to be a lower-cost means of achieving frequency, which is precisely how many advertisers use the medium. Its costs have risen in line with other media, as shown in Figure 1.1.

Magazines

Magazines, like television, are experiencing the problems of decreasing readership and increasing fragmentation. The 1979 edition noted: "General interest publications have all but disappeared, while more specialized magazines have begun to dominate the industry. This movement toward smaller, more manageable audiences, combined with more specialized editorial slants, has enabled magazines to survive despite increases in postal rates and paper costs." This trend has increased during the 1980s.

The possibilities of selective binding, personalized ads, and more demographic and geographic editions are beginning to be exploited, especially by publishers of the remaining mass-circulation magazines in an attempt to compete more directly with special-interest magazines. These large publishers also became aggressive in the 1980s in negotiating ad rates (previously unknown in the magazine world) and offering package deals. In some cases, this has made it difficult for individual and specialized magazines and smaller publishers to get the advertising they need for survival. This competition, together with the recession, has cut the number of new magazines introduced in recent years to half the rate of the 1980s, as well as eliminating some specialized and smaller circulation publications.

The increase in magazine and newspaper rates, as shown in Figure 1.1 has been even greater than that for television in the recent years of the recession.

The 1979 edition of this book contained a passage from Erwin Ephron, given at a *Media Decisions* magazine seminar in 1978, explaining why, in his view, magazines were finding it harder than one might have expected to benefit from the explosive increase in television prices. It is worth repeating the passage in full, since there would still be substantial agreement with it today (Ephron has confirmed in a personal communication that he still holds the same view):

> Certainly advertiser use of magazines has increased. The top 100 advertisers raised their magazine budgets by 23 percent. The top 10 advertisers raised theirs by 5 percent. But the switch to magazines has happened without enthusiasm. Most advertisers (and their agencies) do not believe magazines can substitute for television. This attitude is based upon years of television advertising experience. . . . Magazines are equal or superior to television in every media function except in the real, but elusive, area of "impact,"

however defined. Advertisers consider television more "intrusive," "richer in message content," more "immediate" and, therefore, more "effective."

U.S. advertisers think of magazines as more "efficient," more "personal," perhaps more "authoritative," but "slow-acting" and less "effective."[14]

Ephron went on to point out why he felt magazines had been so slighted and how they might be better used to compete with television:

I suggest magazines do not perform as well as television in the real world because advertisers almost never schedule magazines the way they schedule television. They have no minimum weekly GRP requirements for magazine scheduling and in fact never really examine the audience delivery dynamics of magazines the way they do television. As a result they seldom schedule enough magazine weight within the purchase cycle of a product to produce an immediate effect in the marketplace. . . .

Magazine reach and frequency analysis is usually based upon "the magazine list," a "calendar quarter," or the "total schedule." This produces comfortable levels of reach and frequency, but it is misleading because there is no "time frame" for audience delivery. Reach and frequency goals must be related to the product purchase cycle, usually a much shorter period. Television reach and frequency analysis is almost invariably done on a four-week basis. On a similar four-week basis, most magazine schedule weight would be considered inadequate if it were television.

This last point, about the illusory nature of the reach and frequency derived from magazine readership data and the time taken to achieve actual frequency distributions, has recently been made again, notably in experimental work by the Millward Brown agency:

Exposure to magazine advertising is often very delayed indeed, . . . For the more expensive U.K. women's magazines we found that . . . half of the total exposures to an issue have still to occur 8 or 9 weeks after the publication date. And 15 percent of the exposures occur more than 20 weeks after publication date.[15]

The earlier point—that television is the medium with "impact"—continues to be widely held. Here is a recent comment which chimes in with it, from Richard Kostyra, Executive Vice President/Director of Media Services, J. Walter Thompson:

> Print is hurting more than broadcast (due to the recession) because it has less impact and advertisers are looking to maximize impact. When you start to trim dollars, you get rid of tertiary and then secondary marketing plans. Magazines usually fall into that secondary group. If magazines aren't eliminated altogether, there's a cutback in either pages or books.[16]

There is, however, a contrasting view, which draws life from the increasing fragmentation of the TV monolith. There is an increasing role for media which are highly targeted, to reach a niche or specialist market. Where this is the objective, specialist magazines may have an edge over television. It is not a question of one or the other, but of the need to use a variety of platforms and ways to target in on the niche selected. Here are two quotations expressing this point:

> It will no longer be a matter of buying and selling pages at cut rates (a major issue in the 80's) but rather looking at customized packages between print product and video or cable: Michael Drexler, Executive Vice President, National Media Director, Bozell Inc.[17]
>
> Large media companies will have a great opportunity to restructure so that they can provide (agencies) with highly targeted and mass vehicles in their diverse magazine, cable and television properties: Nancy Smith, Director of Media Services, Young and Rubicam.[18]

THE EFFECTS OF MEDIA COSTS AND FRAGMENTATION ON PLANNING

These increasing trends of cost escalation and fragmentation in all the main media, produce an understandable pressure for more efficient buying. Advertising dollars must not be wasted; advertising must be directed as accurately as possible to those who can be expected to respond. *Targeting* is one way of achieving this; *frequency* may be said to be another.

Professor Charles Ramond set the scene as early as 1976:

> Having decided what to say to whom, and how to say it, the adver-tiser must choose how often he would like each member of the target audience to receive his message. Given a limited budget, there is a necessary trade-off here. He may choose to reach more audience once, or a smaller audience more times. And given his sale or profit objectives, ideally he would like to know the cheapest combination of reach and frequency to achieve those dollar goals. Because pur-chases are induced by communication, in practice the question re-duces to four other questions generally asked in this order:
>
> 1. How many times must an individual be exposed to my adver-tising message for it to have any effect on his subsequent behavior?
>
> 2. In what time interval must these exposures occur?
>
> 3. What number or portion of target audience must I reach with the essential minimum frequency?
>
> 4. On what other conditions do the answers to these questions depend?

In commenting on the importance of finding answers to these ques-tions, Ramond went on to say:

> Clearly, the answers to the first two questions determine the answers to the third. Unless an individual is exposed often enough within a short enough interval, there is little point in reaching him at all. As Zielske's groundbreaking article (1959) has shown, advertising begins to be forgotten immediately after its exposure. Unless the recipient acts upon it almost at once, the ad will have no effect until he is exposed to it again or is otherwise reminded of the message.[19]

This passage from Ramond raises a number of questions that will be addressed in the course of this book. One might question some of the apparent assumptions (e.g., that an ad must be consciously remembered if it is to have an effect). But it expresses well the reason why the understanding of frequency is important to avoiding waste.

Cost per Thousand (CPM), Gross Rating Points (GRPs), Reach and Frequency

Media planners for the last thirty-odd years have continued to rely on cost per thousand (CPM). It appears that, in spite of the availability of single-source and other much-improved data, CPM remains the most-used buying and planning criterion. While there has been much "breathless speculation" about how sophisticated buying may become in the future with all the new facilities, the reality appears to be that little has changed. Much of the more detailed demographic information apparently goes unused even for planning purposes. Supplementary qualitative data, plus judgment, are also important criteria for planning, but not, it seems, quantitative attempts to put different values on various types of impact.

Gross rating points (GRP) have been, and remain, the traditional standard of measurement to provide the units on which CPMs are based. GRPs acknowledge the importance of the *frequency distribution* as well as the *reach* of a medium. They evolved following the rise of television, with its capacity to deliver high frequency relatively quickly.

GRPs are defined as the product of reach and *average frequency:* the percentage of the population exposed to the ad at least once during a defined period of time (reach) multiplied by the average number of times members of the population are exposed during the same period. Thus, for example, an advertiser who bought 240 GRPs during a four-week period could be reaching 77 percent of the population an average of 3.1 times (it could also, of course, mean many other combinations: e.g., 89 percent of the population 2.7 times, or 66 percent 3.6 times).

The "3.1 times" in the above example is of course only an **average,** which covers (usually) a wide **distribution,** made up of some people who are exposed a little, some who are exposed an average amount, and some who are exposed heavily. A typical prime-time television schedule yielding 240 GRPs could look like Figure 1.2.[20]

In this particular distribution, 23.3 percent were not exposed at all; 22.2 percent were exposed once; 17.3 percent were exposed twice; and so on until we see that only .4 percent were exposed 12 times. This perhaps can be seen more graphically in Figure 1.3, where the shaded area under the curve shows the amount of actual exposure involved.

FIGURE 1.2 Frequency Distribution Equal to 240 GRPs for a Prime Time Network Schedule Over a Four-Week Period (Adults 18+)

Number of Exposures		Percent of Viewers		Rating Points
0	×	23.3%	=	0
1	×	22.2	=	22.2
2	×	17.3	=	84.6
3	×	12.5	=	37.5
4	×	8.0	=	34.4
5	×	5.8	=	29.0
6	×	3.8	=	22.8
7	×	2.5	=	17.5
8	×	1.7	=	13.6
9	×	1.2	=	10.8
10	×	0.8	=	8.0
11	×	0.5	=	5.5
12	×	0.4	=	4.8
		76.7%		240.0

240 GRPs ÷ 76.7 Reach = 3.1 Average Frequency

FIGURE 1.3 Total Exposure of a Prime Time Network Schedule Generating 240 GRP's Over a Four Week Period* (Adults 18+)

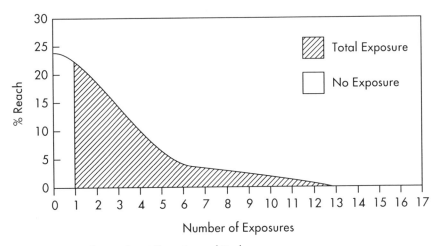

Number of Exposures

* Based on a $6 Million Annual Budget

The GRP calculation, based as it is on *average* frequency, is thus capable of leading to a type of misunderstanding that could be very damaging to an advertiser's purpose. What if the people it is most profitable for him to reach are biased toward the low- or nil-frequency end of the chart? And is a low-frequency delivery good enough for the result required? The problem is compounded with magazines, in which it typically takes longer to achieve a reasonable level of frequency,[21] and with increasingly fragmenting television, which reduces the chance of high frequencies being obtained in short periods from any single channel.

If a media plan is evaluated simply by CPM based on GRPs, with their assumption of average frequency, some fundamental questions relating to how advertising works are ignored. What is the *value* of repeated exposure to an advertising message? Does the second or third in a series of exposures have the same effect as the first? How about exposures beyond three? And what do we mean by "effect" anyway?

By making no explicit judgments on such questions, the media planner implicitly gives each exposure of the advertising message equal value. Thus, the measurement tools of CPM, reach, average frequency, and GRPs, as they have been used in the industry, leave unresolved these critical media allocation problems:

- Is the current media budget being utilized to provide maximum response with a minimum of waste?

- Is the media budget adequate to achieve required results?

- Are funds properly distributed among the media in the mix?

Is There Effective Use of "Effective Frequency"?

The uncertainties and questions raised about the use of simple estimates of reach and frequency, GRPs, and CPMs based on them, were the source of the first edition of this book, which in turn helped to stimulate interest. A study by Turk,[22] reported in 1988, indicated that most media directors surveyed were claiming to use effective frequency concepts in their media planning, at least for some clients. Compared with two earlier studies, the proportion of agencies claiming to use effective frequency in planning rose from 59 percent in 1982, to 86 percent in 1984, to 100 percent (of Turk's 23 respondents) in 1986. In Turk's sample, 61 percent said that 75 percent or more of their clients used effective frequency as a planning element, 17 percent said 50–75 percent of their clients did so, and 22 percent said that less than 50 percent of their clients did so. All claimed that they advised their clients to use effective frequency, and 91 percent said that at least one client asked for it. All claimed to use it (when they did use it) for television planning, and smaller proportions for other media (83 percent for magazines, 39 percent for radio, etc.).

Although Turk's sample can hardly be said to represent the industry fully (half of the agencies invited did not respond to the survey, and we do not know whether, for example, those who did respond tended to be the larger and more sophisticated agencies), this is good evidence of the concept being taken seriously by practical media planners. Nevertheless, there remains an impression that most planners, most of the time, do not use any sort of frequency cell weighting scheme, and do not, in particular, down-weight the higher frequency levels on any assumption of saturation. It is difficult to get a clear sighting of this, but it is probably true that, in practical terms, what is done in most media planning has changed little since the late 1970s, in spite of the growth in awareness of the problems.

The source of this difficulty is not hard to find. Attractive though the concept of effective frequency is, it remains largely ill-defined, and difficult to make real and actionable in a specific media-planning context. It involves assumptions, and the research available, including the new technology of single source data from which so much elucidation has been hoped, has largely failed, so far, to produce the evidence that can clarify and test these assumptions.

As Erwin Ephron described the situation:

> U.S. advertisers seemed to be saying: Since my agency can't tell me how many exposures my message needs to have an effect, I'll make certain I get as many as possible for each dollar I spend. . . .
>
> In the past ten years there has been surprisingly little attention given to basic media questions, such as impact or frequency. For the past ten years media research has focused almost entirely on computer-generated reach and frequency analysis. Endless recomputations of very limited information.[23]

It is possible that he would say the same today. Nevertheless, progress has clearly been made since 1979 in more thinking and better research tools. In this new edition, we attempt to bring the picture up to date, clarify the problems that remain, chart what is now being done in media planning practice and providing research, and suggest where progress can best be made.

The Plan of This Book

Chapter 2 will discuss the concept of *effective frequency* in more detail and highlight those areas where there are conceptual problems as well as difficulties in finding practical evidence. To take the subject forward, we need to understand "frequency of what?" (e.g., the mismatch between "opportunities to see" and actual exposures), "when?" (the implications of different timings, what is meant by "threshold" or "saturation," etc.), and "how do we know it's effective?" (what sort of evaluation counts).

The next five chapters cover the empirical evidence. Chapter 3 describes the psychological basis for the concept of effective frequency and the build-up of laboratory and other experimental evidence. Chapters 4 and 5 deal with the quantitative evidence relating "opportunities to see" television advertising and purchasing behavior, including the London JWT panel experiment of 1966 (McDonald) and the discussions and further studies which have followed it in later years, culminating in the latest work on Nielsen data by Professor John Philip Jones. Chapters 6 and 7 repeat two important early studies, "Ogilvy & Mather" and "AdTel," which appeared in the earlier edition.

Chapter 8, a new section, covers the evidence that has been collected for print advertising—a more difficult field in which to establish clear relationships with behavior, but highly instructive.

After completing our review of the empirical evidence, Chapter 9 will revisit the 12 "conclusions" of the first edition, and investigate to what extent we think they still hold good, or need to be altered or rephrased.

Finally, Chapter 10 takes a brief look at media planning practice, and the use of effective frequency within it. We cannot, of course, claim to cover anything like the totality of what different media planners do, or describe models and programs. That would require a different book—at least as long again—written by professionals in the subject. We merely try to assess the implications of what we know, as we have reviewed it, extract some key principles, and indicate where we hope improvement may come from.

Notes

1. Stephen R. Fajen, "More for Your Money from the Media," *Harvard Business Review* (Sept.–Oct., 1978): 17.

2. E. Papazian et al., "TV Dimensions 1993," *Media Dynamics* (1993): 37.

3. Papazian, p. 17.

4. Papazian, pp. 41, 42.

5. Papazian, p. 55.

6. Cable Television Advertising Bureau, *Cable TV Facts* (1993), p. 7.

7. Cable Television Advertising Bureau, pp. 50–63.

8. Papazian, "TV Dimensions," p. 14.

9. Papazian, p. 27.

10. *Inside Media* (May 2, 1990): 16.

11. Papazian, "TV Dimensions," p. 343.

12. Grey Advertising, "1993 Media Modules" (New York, 1993), p. 16.

13. "Measured Media" *Advertising Age* (Sept. 23, 1992), p. 69. This is the comparable number to the previous edition. If all national advertising, including direct mail, etc., were estimated and added into the base, the percent of television would have been 26 percent in 1978 and 27 percent in 1992, according to McCann-Erickson, as quoted in "TV Dimensions, 1993," p. 22.

14. Erwin Ephron, "The U.S. Advertiser: No Longer a Silent Media Partner," *Media Decisions* (August 1978): 147.

15. Gordon Brown, "TV and Print Advertising," Paper given at the Electronic Media and Research Technologies Workshop, New York, Dec. 1–2, 1992; Advertising Research Foundation.

16. Richard Kostyra, *Media Week* (Sept. 14, 1994): 16.

17. Michael Drexler, *Ad Week* (Sept. 11, 1989).

18. Nancy Smith, *Ad Week* (Sept. 11, 1989): 189.

19. Charles Ramond, "Advertising Research: The State of the Art," (Association of National Advertisers, New York, 1976), pp. 53–54.

20. Alvin A. Achenbaum, "Facing the New Media Reality," Hot Springs, Virginia, Oct. 25, 1977. Part of a joint presentation to the ANA annual meeting.

21. Brown, "TV and Print Advertising."

22. Peter B. Turk, "Effective Frequency Report: Its Use and Evaluation by Major Agency Media Department Executives," *Journal of Advertising Research* (Apr.–May, 1988): 57.

23. Ephron, "The U.S. Advertiser," p. 19.

CHAPTER 2

PROBLEMS WITH THE CONCEPT OF EFFECTIVE FREQUENCY

Frequency is a deceptively simple concept, especially when it is turned into a rule of thumb, such as "three exposures is the optimum number." It is not so easy to apply practically to specific advertising situations, which may be very different. One comes up against the problem of how to define the concept precisely. The difficulty of doing this in a way on which everyone agrees or, more accurately, the range of possible definitions that may quite correctly be applied to different situations, has undoubtedly helped to maintain confusion, and remains an obstacle to the greater sophistication in media planning that still seems so long in coming.

Two quotations, both from the *Journal of Media Planning,* illustrate the frustration:

> Over the years, the search for Effective Frequency has led to no solid conclusions, and for good reasons. The word "frequency" is a catch-all for significantly different advertising effects. Without an understanding of what "frequency" correctly means to a brand, there is little hope of accurately measuring, or even estimating, its effective range.[1]

> • • •

> While many planners use Effective Frequency with no apparent dissatisfactions, there are a number of others who feel that there are many problems with it that either have gone unrecognized, or that have been ignored. The concern is that users of Effective Frequency

17

will either mislead clients into believing that it can do things it cannot do, or misrepresent the facts in some way that will be detrimental to an objective evaluation of media plans. The main misrepresentation is that clients will believe they now know how many advertising message repetitions are needed to make advertising effective.[2]

Such warnings, and they are far from unique, have to be taken seriously. In particular, it is important to read all the evidence about frequency effects, including what is presented in later chapters, with an awareness of just what definitions (and assumptions and limitations) are implied, so that we do not confuse things which are really distinct. In this chapter, therefore, we consider the range of meanings *effective frequency* may have in different contexts, so that it can be kept in mind when we are faced with research evidence which has to be interpreted.

I suggest that there are three main subdivisions within which the meaning of "effective frequency" can vary:

- Frequency of what?
- Frequency when?
- What effects?

FREQUENCY OF WHAT?

What is the thing whose frequency we are studying?

Vehicle Exposures or Ad Exposures?

This confusion has been a major source of controversy. The source of the problem is that the media research data (e.g., readership or audience data) media planners have to use as their everyday currency deliver *vehicle exposure:* a probability that an individual will look at a magazine or a television program containing the advertisement. On the other hand, the theory of effective frequency, at least at the level of psychological response to a stimulus (as developed by Krugman and others), presupposes *actual exposure to the stimulus;* and the laboratory experiments of these theorists have been based on the controlled inducement of such exposures.

The difficulty is not merely that ad exposure is less than vehicle exposure, but that there is no reason to suppose that it is less by a constant amount. The ratio may vary in all sorts of ways, and, since we can hardly even observe actual exposure with any accuracy in real life, it will never be possible to estimate one quantity from the other.

It is even worse than that. There may be several levels of closeness between vehicle and actual exposure. One may know simply what is delivered into a household. With a device like a peoplemeter, one may know that a particular individual was in the room when the TV set was tuned to a particular channel. At this level, we could say that the individual had an "opportunity to see" the commercial; but we still cannot know that he actually did see it. Media research data usually attempt to get as close as possible to "opportunity to see"; average issue readership is interpreted this way, as well as peoplemetered audience research. But there are still possible levels: was the person looking at the box or the page, etc.?

The term *opportunity to see,* or OTS for short, has been regarded as a British term for which the American translation is "probable exposure." They do not really seem to mean the same, however. We suggest that, at least for the purposes of this discussion, "opportunity to see" is to be preferred, not for its Britishness, but because it is simply descriptive: there is an opportunity, which may or may not be taken, and whether it is taken we do not guess. "Probable exposure," on the other hand, seems to carry an implication that an actual exposure was likely, an assumption which is strictly unwarranted, since we have no means of knowing the true probability. OTS tends to be used for all media, although, to be accurate, it should only apply to visual media; the correct term for radio should be "opportunity to hear" (OTH).

The possibility of confusion between vehicle exposure (or OTS, however defined) and actual exposure to the ad has severely concerned a number of critics. For example, Sissors made the following comment:

The fact that there are differences between vehicle and advertisement frequency are well-known among media planners. But for some unknown reason, these differences have not been widely publicized in literature dealing with effective frequency. *Perhaps there are some advertising practitioners who assume that there is so little difference between the two, that it doesn't really matter.* Such persons may assume that there is a one-to-one relationship, which would mean that every vehicle exposure results in a subsequent advertising exposure. But the evidence is clear that a one-to-one relationship is not correct.[3]

Sissors goes on to quote from a speech made by Jack Hill, Director of Media Research at Ogilvy & Mather, at an Association of National Advertisers meeting in 1975.[4] Hill criticized the application of Krugman's three-hit theory, one of the theoretical foundations of the effective frequency concept (discussed in the next chapter) for falling into "the simple, but devastating semantic error" of assuming that the term *exposure* when used by media people meant the same as it did for Krugman. Hill went on to demonstrate, from 1964 data on television commercial exposure, that program audiences were much larger than commercial audiences: his data are reproduced in Table 2.1, which makes the point very clearly (similar differences can easily be demonstrated for print).

Sissors went on to say: "Since these findings show that vehicle exposure is greater than advertising exposure, it is necessary then to know the relationship between the two. Is it constant or variable? Can we predict it? Etc."

There is a school of thought which would argue, in contrast to Sissors's statement above, that since we can measure vehicle exposure and/or OTS with some accuracy, but it is virtually impossible except in the laboratory to get close to actual exposure, there is little point in being too concerned about this admitted difference. If it can be shown that there is a relationship between some measure of response and frequency of OTS, that is the relationship planners have to use and model. What happens in the "black box" between OTS and actual exposure need not be their concern.

TABLE 2.1 Average Performance of Commercials on Programs Telecast in the Evening in Two Markets

	St. Louis		*Chicago*	
Time	7:00–8:15	8:15–9:30	7:00–8:15	8:15–9:30
Household tuned to programs	100	100	100	100
Housewife viewers of programs	65	67	46	56
Exposed to commercials	31	41	33	46

This point of view is enhanced by the evident difficulty of pinning down "actual exposure," even in psychological terms. Krugman developed this point in an article in 1977, in which he responded to comments by Hill and others on his earlier understanding of "exposure" when he was describing the "three-hit theory." He argued that "peripheral perception" (the ability to see something without paying conscious attention to it) is likely to be relevant to advertising, and that measurements of "exposure" based on recall will always underestimate it, so that true "exposure" may well be much closer to OTS than appears from the measurements:

> I conclude that quick and/or faint perceptions of product advertising, even unremembered, do their job in most cases and that the "actual" exposures are closer to the media-scheduled exposures than we give the media credit for. . . . I suggest that ads are meant to be looked at, to communicate as quick as a wink, that 50-percent "noting" probably translates into something over 75-percent actual exposure. . . . The example of television is even more striking. You don't even have to know how to read these. . . . As a practical matter and for immediate purposes, one need not perhaps be too concerned about whether or not exposure can be proven to have taken place. More and more, as an advertiser, I'm willing to assume it.[5]

There is no standard solution to this argument. It is clearly desirable for researchers to improve their ability to pin down "exposure," which implies understanding the different levels of meaning it can have (since there is never likely to be a single agreed definition). At the same time, media planners will continue to have to use the surface measures available to them—of vehicle exposure, or program or page exposure, or even exposure to a commercial break, all providing different levels of OTS. What is important is that those who produce such data, as well as those who use them, should be clear about exactly what is being measured, and how it may perhaps differ from other measurements with which they might wish to compare it. All the evidence in this book needs to be read with this firmly in mind.

Numbers or Share of Voice?

Most of the evidence considers frequency in terms of *numbers* of exposures (or OTS): 0, 1, 2, 3, 4, etc. But this ignores what else is going on in the market at the time. There are good arguments for saying that effective frequency models would make more sense if they were expressed in *category share of voice* terms. In other words, what may matter is not the number of ads transmitted, but whether that number is calculated as an effective proportion of the category. The "threshold" question then becomes, not whether, for example, one exposure is enough, but what share of voice is enough to get attention in the way desired.

This question is closely connected with that of timing, below. The theory of "flighting" is that thereby one will achieve domination (or at least a threshold share of voice) in a limited period.

Different Media

It cannot be assumed that repetitions in one medium have the same effect as repetitions in another. Achenbaum, for example, says:

> The more I have thought about it (and some media people should also have thought about it), I became convinced that it takes fewer exposures for print to be effective than for television. In fact, in print you don't want frequency, you want reach.[6]

The idea here is that people may tolerate repeated viewings or hearings of a commercial, but will not normally read the same ad twice in a magazine. That is debatable, depending on what is in the ad. The point is made that at least we must be aware that there could be differences between media in the relationship between OTS and exposures (opportunities delivered and opportunities actually taken), depending on the subject. There may also be differences within media, e.g., different commercial lengths.

Creative Treatments

An extension to the above is the general point that we are not dealing with nonsense syllables, as in Ebbinghaus's experiments, but real advertisements, which may vary enormously in appeal to an audience according to their subject matter, creative treatment, the recipient's desire for the product, etc. It is unreasonable to expect a simple, universally applicable model of effective frequency, irrespective of the quality of the advertising and the involvement of the audience.

FREQUENCY WHEN?

Timing

Frequency is a strictly meaningless concept except within a defined time frame. Obviously, a frequency of three in one week is not likely to be as effective as the same frequency spread over a month or a year.

> Suppose, somehow, an advertiser could establish that the three-to-six exposure level was "ideal." . . . So far so good. But even if the judgments we have cited had merit, they ignore . . . vitally important issues like timing. When we say that three to six contacts is the "optimal frequency," are we referring to a week, a month, a quarter, or the whole year? Usually the time frame that media planners deal with is limited to a four-week interval, yet this is clearly inappropriate for many products.[7]

If we compare frequencies, we must compare the same time periods, and for those products for which they are appropriate.

Clustered or Spread

Repetitions close together are likely to have a stronger immediate effect than the same number spread apart; we therefore have to consider not only the time frame but the degree of clustering. This point may be obscured by the psychological explanation of the "three-hit rule" (in which it is only at the third exposure that the decision is taken), although Krugman, in explaining this theory, allows for the decay effect of a time lapse: "The same person . . . might see and experience the twenty-third exposure . . . as if it were the second."[8] The Zielske experiment, also described in the next chapter, shows how repetition effects differ when they are tightly clustered in a short period compared to being spread evenly over a longer one. It is, after all, only what we have always known about the difference between flighting (or "burst") and continuous (or "drip") advertising.

Propinquity and the Purchase Cycle

A third related point is how close the advertising is to the next purchase, whether it is clustered or spread. Again, it is the question of the rate of decay, or forgetting, as exemplified in Zielske's experiment. If advertising is effective at all, one would expect it to be more so if the purchase occasion or decision follows soon after, and it should be possible to demonstrate this from research.

The point has been argued in support of maximizing frequency in media planning:

> Since we don't know when any given purchaser makes a purchase decision, the more often we expose a potential customer to a message, the greater is the chance of making a sale by reaching the consumer at the decision point.[9]

This appears to make propinquity an unhelpful consideration for planning:

> An effective exposure frequency related to purchase cycles can be dismissed out of hand. Advertised goods have purchase cycles ranging from weekly to annually, or less often. Are two exposures per week for orange juice no more effective than only two per year for an aerosol rug cleaner?[10]

Nevertheless, some products tend to be bought on regular weekly shopping days, and some have seasonal purchase cycles; where we know these, direction of the advertising to the right weeks or days is possible. It is therefore another factor we need to be aware of in interpreting frequency data.

When we think about the timing of exposures/OTS in relation to the purchase cycle, we stumble upon another ambiguity in the notion of "frequency." Within a purchase cycle, what we are interested in is whether a clustering of exposures in greater numbers increases the probability that the *next* purchase will be of the advertised brand. This is the implication of much of the theory underlying "effective frequency," including the so-called "three-hit rule." But, if frequency of exposures or OTS is measured independently of purchasing, and the frequency happens to be equal to or less than the purchase rate, we are probably looking at something else entirely: a *repetition of single exposures, each of which may be followed by its own purchase opportunity.* These repetitions may build up over time, but without necessarily implying any clustering which might affect the next purchase probability.

It follows that when we are looking at a purchasing criterion, where the purchase cycle matters, it is important to distinguish in which of these two senses "frequency" is being measured. This point will be illustrated in Chapter 8, where we deal with print media, since it affects the interpretation of some of the familiar studies in that area; print media have much slower rates of build-up of OTS than tends to be the case with television. The problem is much less likely to arise when the criterion for "effectiveness" is unconnected with the purchase cycle, e.g., awareness or attitude change.

WHAT EFFECTS?

How do we assess the different frequencies? Ideally sales, of course, but the difficulties of identifying sales effects of advertising are too well known to need repeating here. Shifts in consumer purchase patterns are one possibility; it makes a difference whether they are measured from individual movements on single-source panels or by comparing samples exposed at different levels. There are strong arguments for saying that, where these are available (in many fields, of course, they are not), purchase data must be the best and soundest for our purpose—provided we have analytical or other means for dealing with (separating out) all the other variables which affect purchasing, some of which are much more immediate.

Where single-source purchase data are not available, we have to rely on consumers' recall of or reactions to the advertising message, or awareness of and attitudes to the brand.

All these measurements can be obtained in many different forms. We cannot expect them all to have the same result; for example, awareness of advertising messages may well be more volatile, and fade more quickly, than brand awareness or attitudes, and all will be different for a new brand, a new ad for an old brand, or an ad which has been seen many times before.

Advertising Awareness and Sales

The popularity of *advertising awareness* measures, as used in tracking studies, undoubtedly stems from their tendency to show rapid and marked fluctuations in response which can be related to advertising spending or schedule data. Some media planning software attempts to relate them to "effective reach" (i.e., concepts such as 1+ cover, 3+ cover, etc.). Such movements do not necessarily imply anything about sales or purchasing patterns; individuals can be aware of advertising for things they do not buy and vice versa, and an uplift in awareness can happen without any equivalent uplift in buying or change in image. But it can be valid evidence, for all that, that *something* has happened, that the advertising has made an impact of some sort, however temporary.

If, as so often, the main function of the advertising is to reinforce a steady market share, evidence for such impacts can be valuable. Millward Brown draws a distinction between "advertising awareness measures" (strictly, belief that the *brand* has been advertised "recently" but without any implication that any *particular* advertising has been noticed), and the replay of specific (ideally, brand-involving) impressions or messages from an actual campaign.[11]

Recently, some very interesting evidence has been produced by Millward Brown indicating that it is possible to show correlations between their measure, the "Awareness Index," and short-term increases in sales response.[12] The Awareness Index is defined as "the *increase* in claimed ad awareness produced by 100 TVRs." TVR stands for "television rating point," i.e., the proportion of the viewing population that had an OTS. The Awareness Index is produced by modeling TV ad awareness from tracking studies against TVR weight: "the effects of advertising heritage, forgetting and diminishing returns are all factored out in order to identify the effect of current copy on ad awareness." According to Nigel Hollis, "Over the years, we have come to regard the Awareness Index as a measure of the opportunity to communicate a message about a brand."[13]

Sales response is modeled against advertising (TVRs, allowing for decay in the form of "adstock," taking account of all the other sources of sales variation. A crude plotting of sales response against the Awareness Index shows only a weak relationship. It is made stronger, however, by indexing both the Awareness Index and sales response against the average of the same variables for the same brand; this removes the brand's "inherent elasticity to advertising." The relationship becomes stronger still when "all new claim, product launch and advertised promotion executions" (which draw an out-of-the-ordinary attention to the advertisement) are removed. When these two things were done, 73 percent of the variation in sales effectiveness is found to be "explained" by variations in the Awareness Index.

This is only a start, but it indicates the kind of work that needs to be pursued to increase our understanding of advertising effects and how they can be measured. There are obvious limitations, acknowledged in Hollis's paper. The analysis measures only short-term sales response changes related to short-term movements in the Index (although the author quotes cases where trends into the longer term have been observed). We are still looking at frequently purchased goods. It still helps us little to understand whether advertising is being effective when we do *not* see a short-term lift in sales. We have not learned how this relationship might vary for brands in different market share positions and competitive contexts. But for all these caveats, it seems to take us farther than we have yet been towards understanding the uses of measures of "effect" which are not behavioral.

The general point being made in this section is simply that, when reading the research evidence, we have to understand exactly what it is which is being measured as an "effect." We must not assume that these different measures of effect are "really" measuring the same thing, or that they can be directly compared.

NOTES

1. August B. Priemer, "New Alternatives to Effective Frequency in Media Planning," *Journal of Media Planning* (Fall 1986): 25.

2. Jack Z. Sissors, "Advice to Media Planners on How to Use Effective Frequency," *Journal of Media Planning* (Fall 1986): 3.

3. Jack Z. Sissors, "Confusions about Effective Frequency," *Journal of Advertising Research,* vol. 22, no. 6 (December 1982/January 1983): 34.

4. Jack Hill, "How to Measure Advertising Effectiveness" (or, "Why Three Exposures May *Not* Be Enough"), a talk given at the A.N.A. Television Workshop, February 25, 1975.

5. Herbert E. Krugman, "Memory without Recall, Exposure without Perception," *Journal of Advertising Research,* vol. 17, no. 4 (August 1977): 7–12.

6. Alvin A. Achenbaum, "Effective Exposure: The Subversion of a Useful Idea," *Journal of Media Planning* (Fall 1986): 12.

7. Ed Papazian, "Mediology: The Frequency Fracas," *Marketing & Media Decisions* (June 1986): 85.

8. Herbert E. Krugman, "Why Three Exposures May Be Enough," *Journal of Advertising Research,* vol. 12, no. 6 (December 1972): 11–14.

9. Abbott Wool, "Elements of Media: Frequency vs. Propinquity," *Mediaweek* (July 26, 1993): 19.

10. August B. Priemer, "New Alternatives to Effective Frequency in Media Planning," p. 25.

11. Gordon Brown, "Attention and Memory for TV and Magazines," *Admap* (December 1993).

12. Nigel Hollis, "Television Advertising Awareness and Sales." Paper given at 1994 European Advertising Effectiveness Symposium (run by ASI), Brussels, June 9–10, 1994. See also "The Link between TV Ad Awareness and Sales: New Evidence from Sales Response Modelling," *Journal of the Market Research Society,* vol. 36, no. 1 (January 1994): 41–55.

13. Hollis, "Television Advertising Awareness and Sales."

CHAPTER 3

FOUNDATIONS FROM PSYCHOLOGICAL LEARNING THEORY AND RESEARCH

The early theories about the effects of frequency stem largely from the work of psychologically-trained researchers who explored the subject in a laboratory environment. These researchers quite naturally viewed exposure to advertising as a learning experience for the consumer, and took the view set forth by Stanford University Professor Michael L. Ray:

> The promise of learning theory is simply this. If learning theory indicates how responses are linked to particular stimuli, it can help explain how consumers developed their understanding of the environment and apply it to a variety of consumption acts.[1]

William T. Moran attributes the origins of marketing research in general to psychology in a paper he presented to the European Society for Opinion and Marketing Research (ESOMAR) in 1973. He stated:

> Experimentation and behaviorism are the schools of psychology which I believe had the greatest impact on the field of marketing. Most marketing researchers are acquainted with the connection between the experimentalist, Ebbinghaus, and learning and forgetting curves. Interest in recall measures of advertisements stems importantly from his work, and media scheduling models are based,

in part, on similar time related functions. John Watson, the founder of behaviorism, inaugurated the psychological research function as an accredited activity in advertising agencies. . . .

The growing use of experimental design in recent years, however, can be credited largely to the influence of psychology. The bulk of marketing research practice has arisen from our early fascination with probability, sampling theory and statistics.[2]

EBBINGHAUS

In 1885, Ebbinghaus completed the research that was the basis for the psychological study of learning. Ebbinghaus's research involved just one subject—himself. He made up random lists of nonsense syllables and set out to learn them, keeping records of his progress. He used nonsense syllables to be sure that the items he tried to learn would have no prior association attached to them. He would read them aloud, over and over again, testing himself after each reading by trying to recite the entire list from memory. In this way he explored such problems as the connection between lengths of lists and the number of repetitions required to learn them, as well as the rate at which he forgot them.

His most famous finding is illustrated in Figure 3.1. This shows the number of exposures needed to learn an item on each successive day, and the rate at which the previous day's learning is forgotten. The graph shows that, as the lesson is repeated on successive days, the rate of forgetting slows down, and the number of new exposures needed for relearning is reduced.

The potential application of this result to the "relearning" of a repeated advertising message is obvious, although advertising messages are (usually) not "nonsense" and the effects of previous associations, controlled out in Ebbinghaus's experiments, are likely to be crucial.

ZIELSKE

It was Hubert Zielske who adapted Ebbinghaus's method to the study of repeated advertising exposures. The study took place over a year, and was published in 1959.[3] Although it was based on print advertising, the results could be considered, if anything, even more applicable to television, with

FIGURE 3.1   Relearning and Forgetting (Ebbinghaus)

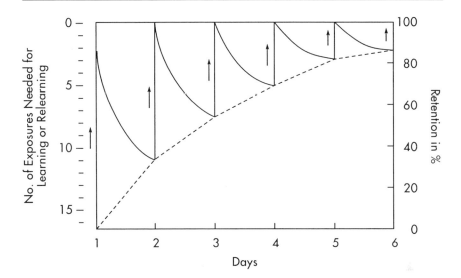

Days

its power to accelerate frequency of exposure; and indeed, later, Zielske and Henry applied a similar analysis to television schedules.[4]

The Zielske experiment was described in a 1966 article by Albert C. Rohloff as follows:

> Briefly, the plan of the Zielske study was to expose one group of women to 13 different ads from the same newspaper advertising campaign at four-week intervals. Every four weeks for a year an advertisement was mailed to women in this group. A second group of women received a total of 13 ads, mailed one week apart. Recall of advertising, aided only by mention of the product class, was obtained by telephone interviews throughout the study, with no single individual being interviewed more than once.[5]

The results are shown in Figure 3.2, in which the two samples are graphed together. It can immediately be seen that the sample who received the advertisements at four-weekly intervals throughout the year describe a pattern very similar to the Ebbinghaus result in Figure 3.1: There is a memory decay after each exposure, but at a reducing rate, and a build-up over time so that, each month, both the level of percentage recall and

FIGURE 3.2 Percentages of Housewives Who Could Remember Advertising, Weekly

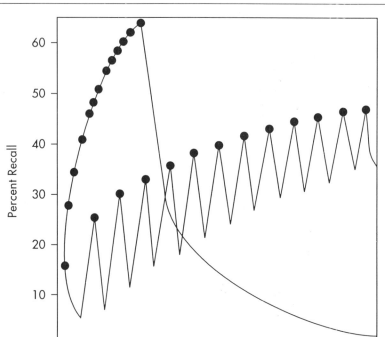

Source: Michael Ray, "Psychological Theories and Interpretations of Learning," *Marketing Science Institute* (August 1973): 4.

the level to which it decays are a little higher than the month before. The other group, which received its ads at weekly intervals and received nothing after week 13, showed a quite different pattern: a rapid rise to a high recall level (at a rate which starts to decline) up to Week 13, and then a rapid fall which declines, by the end of the year, almost back to zero.

Comparing these findings to Ebbinghaus, Ray says:

The fitted curves in the table constitute a replication of Ebbinghaus's findings of exponential acquisition and extinction curves for verbal learning. Despite the fact that the materials and the situation are quite different in Zielske's study from those of Ebbinghaus, the results hold quite well. Furthermore, the effect of the two scheduling treatments in the study is supported by verbal learning research on mass vs. distributed practices.[6]

Methodologically, the difference between what Zielske was measuring and the estimated frequency of distribution from a media plan at that time was the difference between confirmed exposures and an arithmetical assumption. Zielske actually delivered the ads to the homes of the women on his samples; a frequency distribution could only estimate the number who would probably receive each exposure.

It may also be noted that only one exposure, one of either sample, is inadequate to deliver much in the way of recall, and that a concentration of exposures in a short time period has a progressively sharper effect than the more spread out repetition.

Follow-ups to Zielske's Experiment

Zielske's criterion for his mailing experiment was unaided brand recall. In 1980, Zielske and Henry[7] applied the same criterion to the analysis of five television schedules:

- 13 weeks   – 100 rating points
- 26 weeks   – 50 rating points
- 52 weeks   – 5 rating points
- 6–7 weeks   – 100 rating points
- Every 4 weeks – 100 rating points

As with the print study, it was found that the 13-week schedule produced the highest level of brand recall. However, after a year, the 52-week schedule yielded higher scores, again showing the importance of recency.

Zielske's material has been called in evidence a number of times over the question of whether a spaced advertising schedule is more cost-effective than a concentrated one. Simon[8] re-analyzed Zielske's original data to demonstrate that the spaced schedule buys more advertising impact, measured as "recall-weeks" (i.e., the number of weeks multiplied by their recall rates), which he argues is the relevant measure of an advertising campaign rather than the peak recall level achieved briefly: "The total amount of advertising impact (as measured by recall-weeks) is *much higher* for the every-four-weeks schedule than for the weekly schedule." Others have used Zielske's data as a test bed for scheduling models ("pulsing," "chattering," etc.) based on various hypotheses about the implied individual response function.[9]

JAKOBOVITS AND APPEL

The period of the 1960s, following Zielske's work, produced a great deal of introspection and experimentation. Although much of this took place privately within advertising agencies, the most widely discussed and influential studies were published by Appel, Jakobovits, Grass, and Krugman.

Nothing in the Zielske study had suggested that greater frequency might lead to a point of diminishing returns. In 1965, Jakobovits and Appel first suggested this possibility. In separate articles,[10] both men found that if a person is exposed to verbal or visual stimuli, his or her response to learning increases until it reaches a point defined as satiation, and then declines. Jakobovits depicted this repetition result in the form of an inverted U, representing a life-cycle pattern of learning, as follows:

- Generation: Knowledge increases with repetition
- Satiation: Knowledge passes through a maximum and then declines.

The work of Jakobovits and Appel appeared to show that, as a person is exposed to a simple stimulus (such as the meaning of a word repeated many times), his or her response to it increases, passes through a maximum, and then declines, in accordance with this "life-cycle" theory. The inverted U is illustrated in Figure 3.3, which is actually derived from the study by Grass.

GRASS

Robert C. Grass of DuPont undertook some laboratory experiments in 1968 to look for a better understanding of the generation/satiation response pattern as it might relate to advertising. Grass described this work in a paper presented at an ARF Conference in October 1968.

FIGURE 3.3   Generalized Generation – Satiation Curve

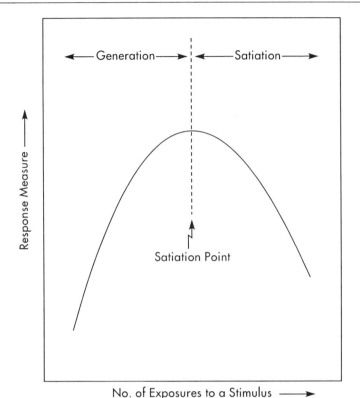

←———Generation———→ | ←———Satiation———→

Response Measure ———→

Satiation Point

No. of Exposures to a Stimulus ———→

The work . . . was conducted by the DuPont Company and Associates for Research Behavior, and it was conducted exclusively with TV commercials. Two criteria of commercial effectiveness were employed. The first of these was a measure of the "attention" or "interest" generated in a subject when he was exposed to a commercial. This measurement was obtained by means of CONPAAD equipment which requires that the subject perform physical work in order to see or hear the commercial. When subjects were exposed to the same commercial again and again on this equipment, a generation–satiation pattern (Figure 3.4) similar to that observed in the work involving simple stimuli was obtained.

Attention or interest was maximized at 2 to 4 exposures of the commercial, depending upon the particular conditions being employed, and was followed by a decline up to the total number of

FIGURE 3.4   Attention Paid to TV Commercials vs. Exposure Frequency

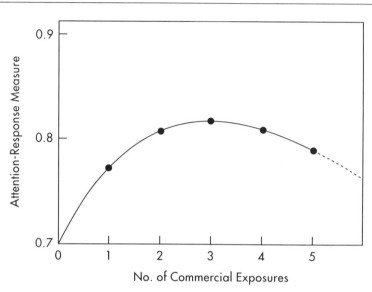

Source: "Satiation Effects of Advertising," Advertising Research Foundation. Proceedings of 14th Annual Conference, New York, Oct. 15, 1968. pp. 20–21.

exposures used in this study. These findings led us to investigate a second criterion of advertising effectiveness—the ability of an ad to communicate with its audience.[11]

The central question Grass was investigating was how many times to run an advertisement. He did not propose that the generation/satiation studies provided concrete answers to such inquiries, but did make the point that the DuPont Company was searching hard to understand effects of frequency in order to better schedule its advertising. Grass went on to comment:

If this relationship is a true one, then we should expect the point of satiation in attention to coincide with or precede maximization of learned information. Fortunately, we can examine this relationship in the case of the Product A and Product B commercials, since these commercials were studied not only from the standpoint of attention (on the CONPAAD equipment) but also from the standpoint of learning in the recall work.

The curves of both the attention and learning responses are superimposed in Figure 3.5 for the Product A commercial. The two sets of data show that, in accordance with the hypothesis we have just outlined, *attention increases and maximizes at two exposures, while the amount of learned information increases and maximizes at two or three exposures.*

A similar situation is suggested by the results from the Product B commercial (Figure 3.6) except that the maximization of information level at exactly the fourth exposure must be hypothetical because of the absence of a data point.

So far, we have confined our attention to communication of facts as a measure of advertising effectiveness, but ads are frequently called on to generate attitudes as well.

FIGURE 3.5   Comparison of Learning and Attention Responses as Number of Exposures is Varied . . . Product "A" Commercial

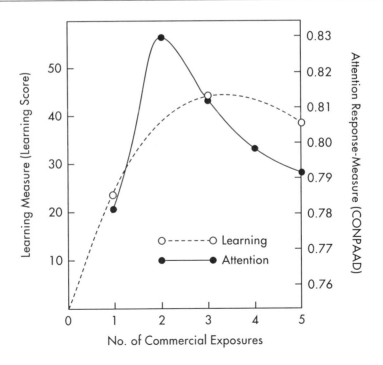

FIGURE 3.6 Comparison of Learning and Attention Responses as Number of Exposures is Varied . . . Product "B" Commercial

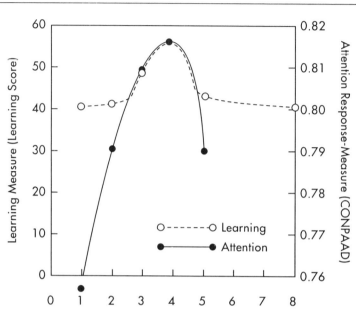

Evidence from another research project involving on-the-air exposure under natural viewing conditions and interviews carried out 24 hours later suggests that generated attitudes are much more resistant to satiation effects than the recall of learned information. Thus, views who saw from zero to eight corporate image commercials over a period of four weeks exhibited attitudes approaching a maximum favorability level for DuPont at three exposures per month, but showed no significant decline in favorability up to eight exposures during that period (Figure 3.7). This differs from the pattern we have come to expect from "learning" in this situation, where we normally see Learning Scores increase to maximum and then decline with increasing numbers of exposures.

Two of the commercials used in this attitude study were the same two corporate image commercials. "C" and "D" used in the satiation study we described earlier, and Figure 3.8 shows the results of these

FIGURE 3.7 Attitudes vs. Advertising Exposures

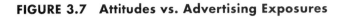

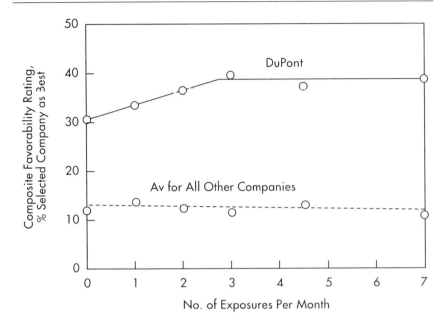

two independent studies plotted on the same graph. The similarity of the data is obvious. Although the low-frequency study involved eight exposures to the two commercials scattered over a month and the high frequency study as many as 19 exposures within five days, the maximum level in both cases was reached at the third exposure. . . .

These studies reported by Grass introduced two new dimensions, *attention* and *attitude,* in addition to *learning a message.* Both attention and learning peak at about three or four exposures under controlled conditions, and then decline rapidly through "satiation" (whatever precisely that is). Attention declines very quickly, suggesting that satiation here means boredom: the mind, once something has been grasped, does not continue to bother with it. Learning also declines from the same point, but less far. There is an interesting difference between the learning curves for Products A and B (Figures 3.5 and 3.6) which is not pointed out in the extract

FIGURE 3.8 Attitudes vs. Advertising Exposures

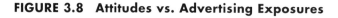

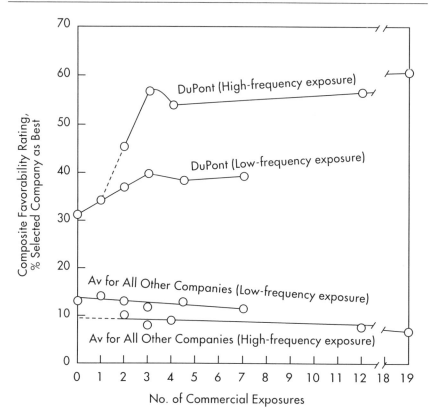

quoted. Product A starts from zero knowledge—presumably it was a new product—but ends at a Learning Score of about 40 (at five exposures), with every suggestion that it will stay up around that level; it certainly seems unlikely to drop back to zero. Product B is already familiar, again with a score of 40, at the start of the experiment; it rises a little (to about 55) with three or four exposures, but then drops back to stabilize again where it was before, at 40. This seems to show that, while attention to stimuli is very volatile, knowledge, once learned, tends to stick at a minimum base level, to which it returns when the stimulus ceases to have an effect. Attitudes are different again. Having been raised, they may remain at the higher level, without dropping back at all.

HEFLIN AND HAYGOOD

Heflin and Haygood, in 1985, in a more recent academic study, tested four levels of spacing (1 day, 1 week, 3 weeks, 5 weeks) of 10 television exposures. The purpose of the study was to extend Zielske's work by bringing *clustering* and *recency* into account, as well as the spacing over different time periods.

The exposures were embedded in television programs which the students were required to watch in a programmed way, so that we are dealing with "real" exposures, not OTS. Unaided brand recall, as with Zielske, was used as a criterion, and also recognition (recall aided by category cues, brand name recognition, and recognition of information contained in the commercials). The brands were taken from three product categories (auto accessories, department stores, and restaurants) which were only available in other parts of the country, thus ensuring that there was no contamination by previous knowledge.

It was found that the two intermediate schedules (1 week and 3 weeks) performed significantly better on all measures than either the 1-day schedule or the 5-week one. This is illustrated in Figure 3.9, for two of the categories.

The authors comment as follows:

The memory curve shown in these data suggests an interplay of two factors: (1) an input factor—satiation, boredom, and avoidance, and (2) a retention factor—forgetting and interference. When advertising is highly concentrated, the amount of satiation, boredom, and avoidance is at its maximum level. As message exposures become less concentrated, this level decreases, but the amount of forgetting and interference increases. Poor performance at one end of the curve suggests that subjects did not learn the material (the input factor). At the other end, it suggests that subjects cannot remember the material (the retention factor). A graphic conceptual model of this notion is shown in Figure 3.10.[12]

This graph appears to give a conceptual explanation for the inverted U curve (the satiation effect) postulated by Jakobovits, Appel, and Grass, when looking at "attention." The study as a whole underlines the importance of *clustering* or *concentration:* satiation occurs fast when too many exposures are too close together.

FIGURE 3.9 Advertising Exposure Schedule – A

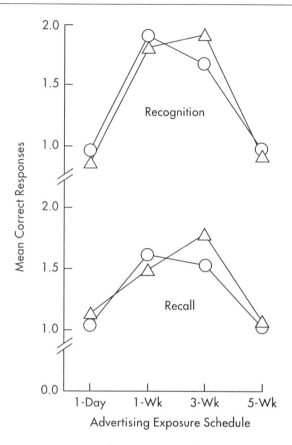

Note: Mean correct responses in the Recognition and Recall tasks as a function of advertising exposure schedule. Data are shown separately for the Restaurant (triangles) and Department Store (circles) commercials.

Source: Debbora Heflin and Robert Haygood, "Effects of Scheduling on Retention of Advertising Messages," *Journal of Advertising,* vol. 14, no. 2 (1985): 45.

Krugman – The "Three-Hit Theory"

Jakobovits, Appel, and Grass were all suggesting, on the basis of laboratory tests (and therefore short exposure periods), that the optimum frequency of exposures for gaining attention and learning a message was about three. This proposition was fitted into a conceptual theory by Dr.

FIGURE 3.10   Advertising Exposure Schedule – B

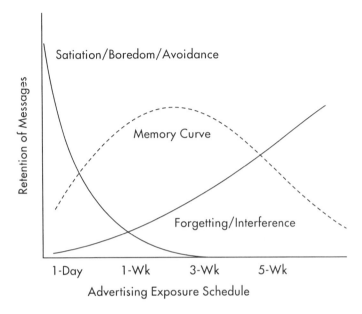

Note: Theoretical model of processes affecting memory for advertisements.

Source: Heflin and Haygood, p. 47.

Herbert E. Krugman of the General Electric Company, who suggested in a presentation at an A.N.A. Television Workshop in 1972 that three exposures to a TV commercial might be the basic minimum number required. Krugman's own words best describe his concept:

> We spend a lot of money on repetition of advertising. Some explain this by noting that recall of the advertising will drop unless continually reinforced, while others note that members of the audience are not always in the market for the advertised product, but that when they are—the advertising must *be there,* so that there's no choice but to advertise frequently. So we can have advertising campaigns of equal magnitude, but based on quite different assumptions about the nature of the effect.
>
> Of course, these two views are apparently quite opposite. One says that the ad must be learned in the same way that habits are

learned—by practice. The other says that at the right moment (when one is 'in the market') it just takes minimal exposure to achieve appropriate effects . . . .

I'd like to offer a view that argues against single-exposure potency, and also against any large number of repeated exposures. I think it is important to understand how communication works and how people learn, and to do that, some attention has to be given to the difference between 1, 2, and 3—i.e., the difference between the first, second, and third exposures. One to make ready, two for the show, three for the money and four to go, or just what? All more complex campaign effects based on twenty or thirty exposures, I believe, are only multiples or combinations of what happens in the first few exposures.

First, I'd like to note that the special importance of just two or three exposures, as compared to a much larger number, is attested to by a variety of converging research findings based on different research methods. In an April 1968 issue of the *American Psychologist,* for example, I reported ("Procedures underlying response to advertising") that an optimal number of exposures seemed to be about two or three. This was based on eye movement data conducted in a laboratory situation, and in response to print advertising. In September 1969, my colleague Robert Glass published a similar finding (three to four exposures) in the *Journal of Advertising Research* ('Satiation effects of TV commercials'), and based on CONPAAD responses to television commercials. . . .

Now let me try to explain the special qualities of one, two and three exposures. I stop at three because as you shall see there is no such thing as a fourth exposure psychologically, i.e., all 4s, 5s, etc. are repeats of the third-exposure effect.

Well, first we have exposure number one. It is by definition unique. Like the first exposure of anything, the reaction is dominated by a 'What is it?' type of cognate response, i.e., the first response is to understand the nature of the stimulus. Anything new or novel, however uninteresting on second exposure, has to elicit some response the first time if only for the mental classification required to discard the object as of no further interest. Thus the new stimulus, good or bad, has an initial attention-getting requirement, even if it is quickly blocked out thereafter.

The second exposure to a stimulus has several implicit qualities. One is that the cognitive 'What is it?' response can be replaced by a more evaluative and personal 'What of it?' response. That is, having now fully appreciated just what is the nature of the new information, the viewer can now shift to a question of whether or not it has personal relevance. Some of this might occur during first exposure if the respondent is absorbing the commercial with great interest, but more likely, especially on television where you can't rewind or reverse the film, there's enough missed first time around so that elements of the cognate reaction are still present on second exposure.

Another element of second exposure, and unique to second exposure, is the startled recognition response: 'Ah ha, I've seen this before!' The virtue of such recognition is that it permits the viewer to pick up where he left off—without the necessity of doing the cognate thing ("What is it?") all over again. So the second exposure is the one where personal responses and evaluations—the 'sale' so to speak—occurs. This "What of it?" response completes the basic reaction to the commercial.

By the third exposure the viewer knows he's been through his "What is its?" and "What of its?," and the third becomes then the true reminder, that is, if there is some consequence of the earlier evaluations yet to be fulfilled. But it is also the beginning of disengagement, of withdrawal of attention from a completed task.

I suggest that this pattern holds true for all larger numbers of exposures. That is, most people filter or screen out TV commercials at any one time by stopping at the "What is it?" response, without further personal involvement. The same person, months later and suddenly in the market for the product in question, might see and experience the twenty-third exposure to the commercial as if it were the second. That is, now the viewer is able to go farther in the nature of his or her reaction to the commercial—and then the twenty-fourth and probably the twenty-fifth—he or she might finish off that sequence with no further reaction to subsequent exposures. . . .

I am not critical of large TV budgets with numerous exposures. I am critical, and the industry will be criticized, if the power of those large budgets is misunderstood or misstated. The large budget is powerful because, like a product sitting on a shelf, you never know when the customer is going to be looking for you, so you must rent the shelf space all the time. But the nature of the customer's reaction is independent, rapid, decisive. He or she makes up his or her mind, perhaps more than once during a campaign, but makes up his or her mind most frequently at some point in the second, or shall we say, psychologically second, exposure to the commercial.

Within this perspective, television advertising plays a modest but important, and thoroughly reasonable, role in the marketing of goods and services.[13]

The importance of Krugman's work, as stated in the above extract and in several other of his writings, is that, besides confirming the pattern of the learning curve reaching its maximum effect with three exposures, which Grass and others had discovered, he gives a very plausible and convincing explanation of it in psychological terms. We can easily recognize it as applying to ourselves in respect of new information in which we might be interested, and equally to advertising which attempts to touch our feelings afresh in connection with things already familiar. It would be difficult to survive in the world without the instinctive screening-out mechanism we all have in our heads.

The other important thing which Krugman does in this passage is to set "exposures" in their long-term, on-going context. He is talking about sets of laboratory-induced exposures occurring close together, and correctly refusing to assume that their effect would be the same, if they were separated in time. A repetition after a space of time would be "as if" it were the second. Timing is crucial to the model.

The other point which has to be remembered throughout is that the first, second and third exposure effects refer to proved exposures, and not to exposures which are merely probable, as is the case with most media estimates. Krugman's own belief in the importance of "peripheral perception," and that there may be less of a gap between opportunities-to-see and true exposures than is commonly thought, has been discussed in Chapter 2.[14]

ZIELSKE AND KRUGMAN — ARE THEY DESCRIBING THE SAME THING?

The different experiments discussed in this chapter appear to point in the same general direction: concentration of stimuli can increase learning, deterioration occurs in the absence of the stimuli, and too much clustering leads to satiation. But one needs to keep one's wits. These experiments are not all measuring the same variables, and there is at least one subtle difference in their meaning that can easily escape notice and has generally done so. This difference is important for the "effective frequency" concept, especially when we come to look at media other than television (Chapter 8). It also involves different potential implications for media planning.

Krugman, following Jakobovits, Appel, and Grass's experiments, is discussing "frequency," in the sense of observing differences in response measured after 1, 2, 3 or more stimuli, in clusters. The timing of these clusters is not fixed, although it is clearly suggested that effects (both of growth and satiation) will be stronger if the clusters are closer together, and there will be a fall-back to some base level if there is a long interval before the next cluster. The key point is that we are looking at the difference between measurements taken *after* 1, 2 or 3 (etc.) "exposures." This is "frequency" as understood in the context of television advertising, where such clusterings of exposures (or OTSs) are possible, and as addressed in the McDonald study and others discussed in the following chapters.

The Zielske experiment is not about frequency in this sense, but about something else which it would be better to call by a different name, perhaps "repeat-rate." Zielske measured the effect on recall of a message delivered at a constant interval, taking his measurements after *each* delivery (i.e., each measurement was taken after *one* further stimulus). His interest was in comparing different *lengths of interval:* Would the rate of growth in recall, and the countervailing rate of forgetting, change if the messages were delivered longer and shorter intervals apart? The Zielske experiment is about the *timings* of exposure, rather than their numbers, and assumes a precisely regulated timing. Zielske and Henry later applied the same principles to comparing television ratings in different, but quite lengthy, time periods.

When we come to look at print media, in Chapter 8, it will be seen that some of the studies most quoted in the frequency debate are, in fact, Zielske-type experiments rather than Krugmanesque ones; only one study makes a genuine comparison of OTS frequencies in print. It could be argued that the Zielske-type approach is more appropriate for print anyway, since insertions have to take place at prespecified (weekly, monthly, etc.) intervals, and the OTS measurement tends to be based on readership of an average issue.

Furthermore, the implications of "frequency" and "repeat-rate" are different. A "frequency" model may suggest that advantage is to be gained by achieving clustering in a small interval of time (e.g., between purchases, or shortly before the next purchase), something which can normally only be afforded by a flighting or "burst" policy. A "repeat-rate" model, on the other hand, strongly points towards a continuous or steady-drip design, with the choice focused on the length of the interval between "exposure" or OTS. This is clearly how Simon in his critique sees it.[15]

NOTES

1. Michael L. Ray, "Psychological Theories and Interpretations of Learning," *Marketing Science Institute* (August 1973): 4.

2. William T. Moran, "Methods of Psychology in Marketing," ESOMAR (June 1973): 2.

3. Hubert A. Zielske, "The Remembering and Forgetting of Advertising," *Journal of Marketing* 23 (March 1959): 239–43.

4. Hubert A. Zielske and Walter A. Henry, "Remembering and Forgetting Television Ads," *Journal of Advertising Research,* vol. 20 (April 1980): 7–12.

5. Albert C. Rohloff, "Quantitative Analysis of the Effectiveness of TV Commercials," *Journal of Marketing Research* (August 1966): 239–45.

6. Ray, "Psychological Theories and Interpretations."

7. Zielske and Henry, "Remembering and Forgetting Television Ads."

8. Julian L. Simon, "What Do Zielske's Real Data Really Show about Pulsing?" *Journal of Marketing Research,* vol. 16 (August 1979): 415–20.

9. V. Mahajan and E. Muller, "Advertising Pulsing Policies for Generating Awareness for New Products," *Marketing Science,* vol. 5, no. 2 (Spring 1986): 89–111.

10. Leon A. Jakobovits, "Semantic Satiation and Cognitive Dynamics." American Psychological Association meeting paper, September 1966. Valentine Appel, "The Reliability and Decay of Advertising Measurements." National Industrial Conference Board meeting paper, October 1966.

11. Robert C. Grass, "Satiation Effects of Advertising." 14th Annual Conference, Advertising Research Foundation, 1968. See also Robert C. Grass and Wallace H. Wallace, "Satiation Effects of TV Commercials," *Journal of Advertising Research* (September 1969): 3–9.

12. Debbora T. A. Heflin and Robert C. Haygood, "Effects of Scheduling on Retention of Advertising Messages," *Journal of Advertising,* vol. 14, no. 2 (1985): 41–47, 64.

13. Herbert E. Krugman, "How Potent Is Television Advertising? Some Guidelines from Theory." A.N.A. Television Workshop presentation, New York, October 11, 1972. See also Herbert E. Krugman, "Why Three Exposures May Be Enough," *Journal of Advertising Research,* vol. 12, no. 6 (December 1972): 11–14.

14. Herbert E. Krugman, "Memory without Recall, Exposure without Perception," *Journal of Advertising Research,* vol. 17, no. 4 (August 1977): 7–12.

15. Ray, "Psychological Theories and Interpretations."

CHAPTER 4

SHORT-TERM EFFECTS OF FREQUENCY ON PURCHASING BEHAVIOR
The McDonald Study

HOW INDIVIDUALS RESPOND TO ADVERTISING

Here is a common-sense scenario of how we *think* advertising probably works on individuals. Each of us, every day, is confronted with a lot of advertising. Much of it is for things we don't buy and never will buy; most of these ads will be ignored, but a few of them we may notice and even enjoy for their own sake (without necessarily deciding to *do* anything as a result). But some of the advertising we see is for things (goods, services, etc.) that we *do* buy or might buy. How do we respond to these?

Sometimes it is possible that seeing an ad may *suddenly* stimulate a new idea, like the little light bulb that lights up over the character in the cartoon. But probably this is rather rare. Much more likely is the reiteration of what is already familiar. Ads, assuming we notice them at all, continuously nudge us, keeping alive the desirable image which is already in our minds, replenishing the emotional strata laid down by all the earlier advertising we have seen before and our experience of the product.

This process is continuous and is the source of the long-term, brand equity building effect of advertising. But it does not make sense to think of this *long*-term effect as distinct (or different in nature) from the *immediate* response which we make to advertising each time we notice it. Much nonsense has resulted from trying to pretend that advertising somehow *only* works in the long term. As John Philip Jones has written: "Two of the conclusions that emerge unambiguously from my own work with single-source research are that (a) an advertising campaign must produce a short-term effect before it is capable of generating a long-term one; and (b) a long-term effect is not guaranteed; it often follows a short-term effect, but not invariably."[1]

The immediate, short-term response to advertising may take a variety of forms: pleased recognition, an emotional lift, amusement, curiosity, possibly a negative reaction (boredom, repulsion). Occasionally (almost certainly in a minority of exposures), seeing the ad may lead to some action being taken, including buying the brand next time if it is a regularly bought category. This last evidence of response may also be affected by other factors, such as consumer offers or price promotions or the strength of competitive advertising, and it would be reasonable to expect these factors to work *together* in guiding the customer toward one brand rather than others, the next time he or she has to think about it.

This view of advertising response is entirely common-sense; that is, it is what one would construct just by looking into one's own experience before examining any evidence from outside. The important thing about it is that it does not assume anything *automatic* or *inevitable* about the response. Not only do individuals differ from each other in what they respond to, but the *same* individuals can vary in their response at different times. People, one would expect, are very volatile in how they respond to the same advertising at different times; it depends on what happens to be uppermost in their minds (or emotions). The carrying through of mental response into buying behavior must be even more volatile still, because other factors then intervene. We might buy more of brand A this week than usual, because it has a deal on in the supermarket, and ads for A might well have reinforced that decision. But it probably means we will buy *less* of A next week (just because we have satisfied our need in advance), and seeing more ads for A will not then make any difference. For an ad to be working, we only have to show that *some* people respond to it some of the time, perhaps quite rarely.

WITHIN-PERSON MEASUREMENT

Unfortunately, that very randomness and unpredictability, and comparative rarity, of response (especially if they are evaluated in terms of buying behavior) make it very difficult to be certain when you *have* got a genuine response, much less measure it in quantity. Putting together the usual aggregate measures of sales, purchases, or attitudes on the one hand and advertising delivery weights on the other simply does not work. It is impossible to be sure, even when there is a correlation, that the sales movement is the result of the advertising and not of some other factor which is confounding the measurement. There is only one way in which it is possible to prove convincingly that advertising has caused behavioral or attitudinal change, and that is to take the measure down to the level of the individual, and find those cases where a person's behavior is different after seeing advertising than it was before; one can then add together these links, established at the disaggregated level, with confidence that we know what the resulting measure means. It is for this reason—the normal aggregate measures not working, and the need for different kinds of measures at the level of the individuals—that many operators have despaired of establishing short-term advertising effects, or even doubted that they exist, and concentrated so heavily on the long term.

But can short-term effects, at the individual level, be observed and measured? Yes, they can, if we have the right data. The data needed are what Jones has called "pure single-source research," defined as follows: "pure single-source research determines each household's reception of advertising for specific identified brands, and it relates this to the purchasing of those same brands in the same household shortly after the advertising."[2]

THE MCDONALD STUDY

The first attempt to carry out such research, on a pilot scale, was in an experimental project commissioned by J. Walter Thompson, Limited (London). This project was originally proposed and directed by Timothy Joyce, a director at that time of the British Market Research Bureau Limited, a subsidiary company of JWT London. The format of the study and the rationale of some of the data collection methods used are described in a 1967 paper by Joyce. In it, Joyce makes a point which has tended to be forgotten in the subsequent debate: "The main reason for undertaking this project was to throw light on advertising problems rather than media problems."[3]

A diary was kept over 13 weeks among housewives in the London ITV area at the end of 1966. Completed diaries were obtained from 255 housewives. On each day, the housewives recorded their purchases in 50 different product fields, the issues they had seen out of 32 newspapers and magazines, and the ITV segments they had seen with each program segment and commercial break separately identified.

The purpose of the experiment was to gain a deeper insight into housewives' patterns of purchasing in relation to their opportunities to see advertisements (OTS). OTSs were derived by collating the detailed reading and viewing information in the diaries with known insertions and transmissions of commercials for the different brands (a service easily available in the UK where, at the time, there was only one commercial television channel). The panel was thus, in Jones's terms, "pure" single-source data.

The raw material that could be derived from the diary consisted of a day-by-day record of purchases and OTS for each person. Table 4.1 shows an example of one of these records for breakfast cereals, the code letters referring to different brands.

To put this complex data set together in such a way as to derive useful information from it involved developing new methods of analysis. This task was undertaken by Colin McDonald, who was then at the British Market Research Bureau and was responsible for the design and execution of the analysis and its reporting in various papers.

McDonald analyzed 9 of the 50 product fields from the diaries and reported the findings in two papers. The first, based only on the first three product categories analyzed, was delivered at the Market Research Society Conference in Britain in 1969.[4] The second was given at the ESOMAR

TABLE 4.1   Example: Part of One Person's Data on Cereals

Days:	Sep	20	21	22	23	24	25	26
		Tue	Wed	Thu	Fri	Sat	Sun	Mon
Purchases:		J	—	Q	—	—	—	G
OTS:		C		C	C	C		
		F			F			F
		J	J		J			J
		O	O	O				
			G	G			G	G
			Y					
					B	B		

(the European Society for Opinion and Marketing Research) Conference in 1970.[5]

The ESOMAR paper was republished in the United States by the Marketing Science Institute and promptly became evidence quoted in the debate about effective frequency. It was published again in the first edition of this book. The reason for this was that the results were able to demonstrate convincingly that advertising did have a short-term effect, and moreover, that it appeared to follow the "effective frequency" hypothesis: the strongest effects appear after 2 OTS, increasing at 3 or more but at a diminishing rate, whereas, apparently, after only one OTS, effects seem to be negative (which means that the brand advertising at this level is "beaten" by competitors with a heavier weight). These findings appeared to support the psychological explanation of Krugman, that messages are not fully grasped until at least the third exposure, and were influential in the development of the so-called "three exposures" rule.

In certain respects, however, the findings of the McDonald study have been misunderstood, and their correct interpretation does not quite support the weight of dogma that effective frequency theorists over the years have heaped upon them. Partly, this occurred because of the particular emphasis given to the 1970 paper (the one that became widely known), in order to demonstrate that a genuine, not spurious, short-term effect of advertising could be observed and measured (something not known before); possible uses for media planning were not the objective of the paper. The author welcomes the opportunity now to set the record straight, on such matters as the famous S-shaped response curve.

The following sections summarize the analyses from both these papers and the reasoning behind them.

The First Analysis

The question for analysis was, how to find a valid relationship between the two "time series" of ads and purchases. Simply relating the aggregate numbers together gives a spurious matching driven by weight: the heavier buyers also see more TV and therefore more ads (for everything). The relationship had to be *within individuals*.

An important constraint is that a causal relationship, if it exists at all, must point *forward* in time. Change toward a brand must be more likely *after* advertising has been seen than *before,* if we are to say that there is a short-term effect. The first investigation therefore looked at three product categories where two successive purchases of the same brand were followed by a change—i.e., people had followed the purchasing sequence A → A → B. The three product categories were washing detergents, cereals, and tea.

If a short-term effect is operating, we would expect to find that there were relatively more OTS for B, on average in the *second* interval (when A → B) than in the first (when A → A); conversely, there would be fewer OTS for A in the A → B interval than in the A → A one. When we aggregate all these cases we find the results shown in Table 4.2.

A marginal effect of the kind we have hypothesized exists. In all the six rows except the last one, there are more "B" OTS, and fewer "A" OTS, in the second interval than the first. "B" OTS are associated with later switching *to* "B:" "A" OTS are associated with *not* switching away from "A."

The Main Analysis: CHANGE and REPEAT Measures

This first-line evidence that we were seeing short-term effects led to a more general analysis using the *purchase interval* as the unit analyzed. You can, of course, only do this with categories which are purchased fairly frequently. A *purchase interval* is any two successive purchases and the space between them, which may or may not be filled with advertising OTS.

Let us consider a Brand X (which can stand for each of the individual brands in a product field in turn). The people who will give us useful information for switching analysis are those who buy Brand X *and* at least one other brand in the course of the panel. All other brands bought which are not X are called Brand O.

TABLE 4.2   Sequences Where Two Purchases of the Same Brand Are Followed by a Switch (A → A → B)

		First Interval (A → A)	Second Interval (A → B)
Washing Detergents	OTS "B"	110	128
	OTS "A"	166	157
Cereals	OTS "B"	140	150
	OTS "A"	184	174
Tea	OTS "B"	60	76
	OTS "A"	55	64

In terms of Brand X, an individual can have only *four* kinds of purchase interval:

Switching intervals:	to X (O → X)
	away from X (X → O)
Loyal intervals:	X → X
Non-buying intervals:	O → O

For each brand, these intervals can be cross-tabulated against the occurrence of OTS for X, thus:

	OTS for X in interval					
	0	1	2	3	4	etc.
O → X						
X → O						
X → X						
O → O						

Table 4.3 shows how this counting procedure works for the cereals example in Table 4.1.

In this example, the housewife had 2 OTS for G before she changed to G, 1 before she changed away from G and in her other intervals, when she did not buy G at all, had respectively 3 OTS once—one once and none twice.

This counting is done for each brand in turn, and the resulting tables are added to produce a composite Brand X. It will be noticed that each "switch" interval will be counted twice: an interval A → B will be taken both as O → B and A → O. Double or treble purchases on the same occasion are counted separately for each brand.

The analysis was done for nine separate product categories: the three above (washing detergents, cereals, and tea) plus: wrapped bread, soups, shampoos, toothpaste, milk drinks and margarine.

From these tables of purchase interval type against number of OTS, one can calculate certain ratios that reveal whether there is an effect or not:

1. The ratio O → X/O → X + O → O. This has been named TRIAL (or, perhaps better, CHANGE), i.e., the proportion of all intervals starting with a *different* brand that *end* with Brand X. If this proportion *increases* from left to right of the table (i.e., when there are

TABLE 4.3 One Respondent's Cereal Record

Purchases:	J	Q	G	H	L	F	A
OTS		2J	1J	1J			
in intervals		**1G**	**2G**	**1G**			**3G**
		1f	1F	3F	4F		
		1C	3C	1C	4C	1C	1C
				2R	4R		2R
						1T	1T

Counting **G** we find: OTS in Interval

	0	1	2	3	4+
O → G			1		
G → O		1			
G → G					
O → O	1			1	

more OTS for X in the interval), we can say that this shows the *attractive* power of the advertising *toward* the brand.

2. The ratio X → X/X → X + X → O. This has been named REPEAT, and is the proportion of all intervals *starting* with X which *remain loyal* to X at the second purchase. If *this* proportion increases when there are more OTS for X, it is a measure of the power of advertising to keep existing users loyal, i.e., its *retentive* effect.

These ratios for the nine categories were as shown in Table 4.4. In almost every case, apart from the two that have been starred, there was a higher likelihood both of changing to or staying with the brand when at least two OTS for that brand had occurred, than when there had been only one OTS or none.

If we aggregate the nine categories, instead of averaging them as in Table 4.4, we can enlarge the sample enough to show the OTS broken out in more detail. This can be seen in Table 4.5.

From this table, it is clear how both the CHANGE and the REPEAT variables increase in likelihood with even *one* OTS, increase again with

TABLE 4.4   % "CHANGE": O → X Out of All O → INTERVALS

OTS in interval	0,1	2+
	%	%
Washing detergent	20.8	29.0
Cereals	17.8	25.6
Tea	16.9	24.2
Soup	26.2	29.3
Margarine	23.3	27.9
Wrapped bread	12.7	20.0
Toothpaste	32.8	41.4
Shampoo	29.4	37.8
Milk drinks	<u>37.1</u>	<u>42.2</u>
Average	24.1	30.8

% "REPEAT": % X → X Out of All X → INTERVALS

OTS in interval	0,1	2+
	%	%
Washing detergent	57.9	67.5
Cereals	32.6	51.3
Tea	61.9	73.2
Soup	66.6	65.9*
Margarine	70.8	72.6
Wrapped bread	59.4	66.1
Toothpaste	50.4	60.0
Shampoo	48.1	36.4*
Milk drinks	<u>51.6</u>	<u>55.9</u>
Average	55.5	61.0

two, and how the curve tails off at three or more. It also shows greater instability because of the decreasing sample bases. We need to remember always that it is more common for consumers *not* to see our advertising, even when they are heavily exposed to TV.

If the figures are averaged over the nine categories instead of being aggregated, they differ in detail, but the general picture is the same.

TABLE 4.5   Nine Product Categories (Aggregated)

	OTS in interval				
	0	1	2	3	4+
Number of intervals	24,897	4,809	2,039	894	966
	100%	100%	100%	100%	100%
Type of interval	%	%	%	%	%
O → X	12.5	13.3	16.7	14.9	18.0
X → O	12.4	15.1	14.5	13.3	17.1
X → X	14.8	21.2	24.4	27.4	24.8
O → O	60.3	50.4	44.4	44.4	40.1
CHANGE	%	%	%	%	%
(O → X / O → X + O → O)	17.1	20.9	27.3	25.1	31.0
REPEAT	%	%	%	%	%
(X → X / X → X + X → O)	54.4	58.4	62.7	67.3	59.2

We would draw attention to the fact that, in Table 4.5, *the REPEAT progression shows a convex response curve, not an S-shaped one, and the CHANGE progression only shows a slight S-shape.* The percentage increases between each level of OTS are:

		CHANGE	REPEAT
OTS:	0 – 1	+ 22%	+ 7%
	1 – 2	+ 31%	+ 7%
	2 – 3	– 8%	+ 7%
	3 – 4+	+ 24%	– 11%

In the 1970 paper (the one circulated by the Marketing Science Institute), the collapsed figures in Table 4.4 were given, but not the expanded figures in Table 4.5. With hindsight, the author regrets this, since it might have helped to avoid some of the misunderstanding that has attached to the S-shaped curve shown in the paper in relation to the SWITCH variable. The reasons the paper concentrated on the SWITCH variable will, we hope, be clear from what follows.

Conceptually, it is not too difficult to explain why a measurement of CHANGE into a brand might have a mildly S-shaped response function, while a REPEAT purchase measurement has a convex one. Repeat buying occurs predominantly among the brands with larger shares, which are not only bought by more people, but also bought more frequently, and with a history of relatively frequent and familiar advertising. One ad is quite likely to be enough in many cases to act as a stimulus. Trial occurs with newer, smaller share brands, which may need more effort to get past the competition, and newer or less familiar campaigns that may fit Krugman's perceptual model more neatly.

The SWITCH Variable

Another ratio, called SWITCH, was also calculated. This used *only* the switching occasions, and calculated O → X as a proportion of O → X + X → O (i.e., the proportion of all switches *to* or *from* X which are *to X*), ignoring any other purchase occasions (i.e., X → X or O → O). This is the analysis given most emphasis in the 1970 paper, for the following reason.

The particular value of the SWITCH measurement is the tight logic imposed by the fact that *in any individual sequence of purchases, the number of O → X and X → O intervals are by definition equal,* plus or minus one depending on the cut-off point of the sequence. Thus, the Null Hypothesis must be that, if advertising has no effect, the ratio of switches to to switches from must be 50:50 at all levels of OTS. If the ratio grows with the number of OTS, it cannot be due to any self-selection of respondents (e.g., those who see more advertising being more likely to switch to the brand), since *every* respondent's switching into and out of Brand X is equal in number of occasions. This tight logic is not strictly true of CHANGE and REPEAT. For example, it *could* be the case that highly loyal buyers are more likely to have sequences of X purchases (i.e., X → X most of the time, but much less often O → X or X → O), whereas more promiscuous buyers have relatively fewer X → X and more O → X or X → O intervals; if the advertising was successfully being targeted disproportionately to the loyal buyers, it would follow that *different people,* who were receiving different amounts of advertising overall, could be appearing in the X → X, O → X or X → O, and O → O counts, and this could affect the distribution appearing in the REPEAT and CHANGE formulas. With SWITCH, because of the precise balance of to/from switches for each person and each brand, this would be impossible.

For practical purposes, the CHANGE and REPEAT measures are more useful for media planning and, in spite of the above proviso can be used with some confidence. In these categories, most buyers are multi-brand buyers (and indeed, single-brand buyers were excluded from the analyses), and the more they watch television, the more they see advertising for *all* the competitors. One would have to be very clever at targeting to single out only buyers of Brand A and ensure that only A's advertising is delivered to them. In the paper, interest was centered on SWITCH, because the aim was to show that advertising effects could be truly observed, that the relationship was not spurious; in practice, SWITCH should probably be seen as useful confirmatory evidence to back up the other measures.

The SWITCH figures calculated from Table 4.5 are shown in Table 4.6.

The same general trend applies to each of the product categories, as shown in Table 4.7 (analogous to Table 4.4).

Table 4.6   Nine Product Categories Aggregated

	OTS in interval				
	0	1	2	3	4+
SWITCH	%	%	%	%	%
$(O \rightarrow X \,/\, O \rightarrow X + X \rightarrow O)$	50.2	46.8	53.5	52.8	51.3

Table 4.7 % O → X Out of All SWITCHES (i.e., O → X + X → O)

No. OTS IN INTERVAL	0 or 1	2 or more
	%	%
Washing detergents	49.6	52.4
Cereals	49.8	51.3
Tea	48.1	62.8
Soup	49.4	52.2
Margarine	49.9	51.0
Wrapped bread	50.2	56.3
Toothpaste	47.4	54.7
Shampoo	47.6	50.0
Milk drinks	<u>53.7</u>	<u>55.9</u>
Average	49.5	54.1

In Table 4.6, the response function is an S-shaped curve with an unusual shape. At 0 OTS, the ratio of *switches to* to *switches from* is 50:50, as one would expect from the Null Hypothesis. At 1 OTS, the ratio *drops below* 50, to 47:53. At 2 OTS, it rises sharply, to 53.5:46.5, and at higher levels of OTS it tails away, while remaining above 50.

This S-shape has been more influential than it deserves, having been quoted in support of the proposition that advertising, to be effective, must deliver on average at least two opportunities to see before a purchase (often the argument slides into "exposures"), and that one alone is insufficient. It is important to be clear why it occurs in this measure only.

There are two reasons. One is an artifact of the particular form of analysis used. The 50:50 balance between switches *to* and switches *from* applies to *each* brand within *each* individual, and therefore by extension over all brands and all individuals. It is easy to demonstrate this by an example. Here is an unusually complex buying pattern, from a real consumer in the tea market (each letter is a different brand):[6]

P E B P P G I I P P G K P P A P P

If we pick out the *switches to* and *from* each brand, we get:

Brands	To (O → X)	From (X → O)
P	4	4
E	1	1
B	1	1
G	2	2
I	1	1
K	1	1
A	1	1
Total	11	11

However simple or complex, the same applies to any purchasing sequence.

Since the ratio is 50:50 overall, it follows that if, at 2 or more OTS, it rises *above* 50, this rise must be balanced by a drop *below* 50 elsewhere. The balancing drop at 1 OTS is thus an inevitable artifact of the analysis designed to yield an expected 50:50 ratio. One could write:

Number of OTS IN INTERVAL	0 or 1	2 or more	Total
	%	%	%
Expected	50	50	50
Actual	49.5	54.1	50

This leaves two questions. First, why are the balancing figures not equal: 54.1 (+ 4.1) does not balance 49.5 (– 0.5)? The reason is that we are looking at percentages, on very different bases. As can be seen in Table 4.5, the numbers diminish rapidly as one moves from left to right of the table. This is because, even in a heavily advertised field, most people do not see advertising most of the time. The same number, on a larger base, gives a smaller percentage. If we were looking at raw numbers instead of percentages, they would balance exactly.

The second question is, why is the percentage figure lower at 1 OTS than at 0 OTS? When people see advertising for our brand, they also tend to see it for the competition. A large number of the 0 OTS intervals are times when *people were watching little or no television anyway,* and therefore were not seeing *any* advertising. When they *are* watching, they tend to see all the brands on the box. This brings us to the practical reason for the S-shape. The seesaw effect we see, with 1 OTS going down as 2+ OTS goes up, is due to brands with 2 or more OTS "winning" over brands with only one, at times when both are being received. It is worth remembering also that OTS does not necessarily imply exposure: sometimes 2 OTS will mean only 1 exposure, and 1 OTS no exposures, etc.

It is hoped that this lengthy explanation will put the S-shaped curve into a truer perspective, not as a universal truth but as something revealed and explicable when the evidence is looked at in a particular way. The value of the approach is the convincing demonstration it gave that advertising does have genuine short-term effects which can be observed and measured.

OTS Brand Share

Another analysis, done for only one product category (washing detergents) found that the same trends occurred if OTS are expressed in *brand share* terms instead of simply as numbers: this is to be expected if two or more OTS tend to "win" over one, and is a useful confirmation. See Table 4.8.

Effects of OTS in a Short Period

The above analyses were all based on counts of OTS in an entire purchase interval, which might have lasted from a day or two to a couple of weeks or more. But it seemed reasonable to expect that OTS received *shortly* before a purchase may have a stronger effect. Longer purchase intervals (e.g., more than a week) have more opportunity to contain large numbers of OTS (3 or more), yet the effect of these larger numbers could be diluted by being spread over a longer period; this could be the explanation of the apparent "drop" in effectiveness with 3 or 4+ OTS.

TABLE 4.8   Share of OTS Which Are for X

	0–.10	.11–.20	.21–.30	.31–.40	.41+
CHANGE	17.4	28.8	24.1	25.0	35.8
REPEAT	61.6	67.3	69.5	64.2	68.4
SWITCH	39.2	52.3	54.7	49.1	55.9

TABLE 4.9   Number of OTS for X in 4-day Window (Nine Product Categories Aggregated)

	0	1	2	3	4 or more
Number of intervals	27,487	4,228	1,142	380	204
	100%	100%	100%	100%	100%
	%	%	%	%	%
Type of interval					
O → X	12.7	13.5	16.6	16.3	16.2
X → O	12.8	14.7	12.3	12.9	13.2
X → X	15.6	22.1	25.1	23.2	26.5
O → O	58.8	49.7	46.0	47.6	44.1
	%	%	%	%	%
CHANGE	17.8	21.4	26.5	25.5	26.9
REPEAT	54.9	60.0	67.1	64.3	66.8
SWITCH	49.8	47.9	57.4	55.8	55.1

To check this hypothesis, a count was done in the same manner in which the OTS counted were limited to a "window" of 4 days before the second purchase in the interval. The results showed that, indeed, the effectiveness was a little stronger at the higher OTS levels, especially for the REPEAT variable, although the general shape of the response was not altered, it was still the case that the effect levelled off after 2 OTS. This can be seen by comparing Table 4.9 with Tables 4.5 and 4.6.

SUMMARY

These results from the J. Walter Thompson experimental panel seemed to confirm a number of hypotheses about the purchasing of fast moving consumer goods, which were being formulated on other grounds at about the same time.

They showed that it was rare for consumers to "change brands" in a drastic manner: rather, most consumers had a repertoire of a few (sometimes many) brands, among which they would interchange.

With at least some consumers, one could perceive directly that these switching patterns were related to opportunities to see advertising: buying probabilities grew up to a certain level of OTS before the purchase occasion, but tended to level off after about three OTS; and the effects appeared to be stronger when the OTS occurred only a short time before the purchase.

It is important not to overstate what these findings mean. They are *evidence* that advertising is "working" in the sense that buying consumers are responding to it. Only some consumers, and only some of the time, respond in this visible way by actually changing their behavior immediately after advertising; but that does not mean that the others, who do not switch in this obvious way, are not also responding—we infer that, to some extent, they are. We still know very little about what is going on, and how it varies between brands, with different sorts of products and consumers, or how advertising interacts with other types of promotion. We do not have a "model" of advertising working, still less a predictive model for future sales. Much more investigation is needed before these aims can be reached.

All we do know—but it is a significant piece of knowledge—is that it is possible, by analyzing panel data longitudinally within respondents, to observe advertising *as it is working*. That means we should be able to identify a brand where the advertising is effective and distinguish it from another brand where the advertising is failing, even when market conditions are such that it is not possible to differentiate them in terms of short-term movements in sales. It should also be possible to relate observable short-term working with the long-term, brand-equity–building effectiveness of the advertising.

NOTES

1. John P. Jones, *When Ads Work: New Proof That Advertising Triggers Sales* (New York: Lexington Books, 1995).

2. Jones, *When Ads Work.*

3. Timothy Joyce, "Examples of Experimental Work with Media Panels," *Admap* (Sept. 1967): 347–52.

4. Colin McDonald, "Relationships Between Advertising Exposure and Purchasing Behaviour." Market Research Society Conference, 1969, pp. 67–98.

5. Colin McDonald, "What Is the Short-term Effect of Advertising?" ESOMAR 1970, also *Admap,* vol. 6, no. 10 (November 1970): 350–56, 366. Also in *Market Researchers Look at Advertising, A collection of ESOMAR papers 1949–1979,* Ed., S. Broadbent. (Sigmatext, 1980): 39–50.

   Note that in References 3 and 5, "exposure" was being used, strictly incorrectly, instead of "opportunities to see." We have all now tried to tighten up our language. At the same time, in the McDonald study (the study referred to in both of these references), there is reason to believe that the gap between OTS and actual exposure was probably not very great; an OTS was only postulated where the diary panelist claimed to have watched an actual commercial break, or looked at a specific issue of a publication.

6. Barnes, Michael, "The Relationship Between Purchasing Patterns and Advertising Exposure." J. Walter Thompson Company Limited, London, September 1971, p. 8.

CHAPTER 5

WHAT FOLLOWED THE McDONALD STUDY

LIMITATIONS OF THE McDONALD STUDY

The McDonald study was a relatively small-scale experiment. It provided basic evidence that one could observe short-term effect but left many questions unanswered. In particular, there were clear indications, although they were based on samples too small to justify quotation, that the measures would discriminate between different brands with more or less successful advertising, and that they would apply to different media.

Several attempts were made between 1970 and 1978 to obtain funding for a larger scale repetition of the J. Walter Thompson panel, culminating in an initiative sponsored by *Newsweek* which in 1977 sought to raise enough subscriptions to underwrite a one-city pilot in the United States. None of these efforts attracted sufficient interest to proceed.

However, the findings were interpreted as confirmation of the "effective frequency" thesis, especially because they appeared to chime so well with Krugman's "What is it? What of it? Reminder" explanation of the way communications are absorbed. There were other results which appeared to fit. For example, a certain major advertiser analyzed 38 brands over a four-week period, using change in unaided brand advertising awareness as a measurement criterion. This advertiser, from measurements involving almost 3,000 respondents, found that brand advertising awareness over a four-week period did not attain a sufficiently positive level until three exposures were received. In other words, the net result was to show that the countereffects of short-term memory and longer-term

forgetting are—for most packaged goods over an average purchase cycle—
tilted decisively in favor of positive brand response at a minimal level of
three exposures, whereas above three the effects level off.

The analysis used for this advertising awareness measurement was to
calculate the percentage switching awareness into each brand as a percentage of the total switching in and out over the four weeks (i.e., $O \rightarrow X/$
$O \rightarrow X + X \rightarrow O$, the same as in McDonald's SWITCH analysis but using
awareness change instead of purchase change), and compare between
different exposure levels. Because the unaided awareness measures were
taken several times during the four weeks among the same people, it
follows that the proportion switching into and out of each brand must be
equal for each individual, as with the purchase data. The results are shown
in Figure 5.1. It can be seen that the same general pattern is described,
with a sharp increase between 1 exposure and 3; the only difference is
that the 0 exposure level is also below 50 percent, unlike the purchase data.
It must be remembered that we are looking at true exposures here, not OTS
as with the purchase data.

JWT/TVS 1984 STUDY

In late 1984, in Britain, TVS, and J. Walter Thompson Limited commissioned AGB to conduct a 13-week panel study that combined purchasing
and television viewing. The results of this study were published by Phil
Gullen (then Media Director at JWT London) and Hugh Johnson (then
at TVS) in various papers in *Admap*[1] and in the most definitive paper
delivered at an ESOMAR seminar in Helsinki in 1986.[2]

The data used were not as detailed as in the McDonald study. Purchase
data were obtained from an ongoing AGB panel, the Television Consumer
Audit, which reported only on a weekly basis; it did not provide a
breakdown of what people did by day of week. Television viewing was
derived from housewife-completed quarter-hour viewing diaries kept by
the same TCA panel members over the 13 weeks. To align OTS with
purchases, the analysts made an assumption: that "on average any OTS
delivered between the Thursday prior to the TCA week and the Wednes-
day during the week will have been received before the purchase was
made. We arrived at this lagging after considering the purchasing pattern
by day of week in the TVS area, which shows a bias toward Thursday,
Friday, and Saturday." It was estimated that this inaccuracy led to 10
percent compensating errors in both directions.

**FIGURE 5.1 McDonald SWITCH Analysis Compared with a
SWITCH Analysis Using Advertising Awareness as Criterion**

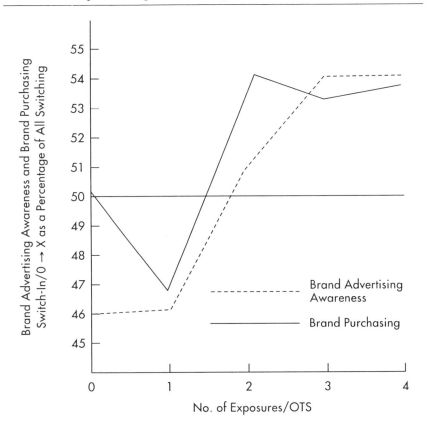

When an attempt was made to replicate the McDonald SWITCH analysis, a similar shape was found but a much less clear-cut result: at 0 OTS,
the switch-to ratio is just over 50 percent, as before, drops to about 48
percent with 1 OTS, and rises to about 52 percent at 2 OTS. However,
above 2 OTS the graph diverges: at 4+ OTS the switch-to percentage is
only just above break-even, at 51 percent, and at 3 OTS it actually drops
below, to 49 percent. These are levels consistent with the Null hypothesis
(virtually no effect, fluctuating around 50). The authors' explanation is
"the timescale over which OTS are delivered." Over the 15 categories
studied, on average, the people having two OTS between purchases will
have seen them during the course of one week, but three OTS were
generally delivered over longer periods. This is in contrast to the earlier

study, in 1966, when "weekly strike rates for grocery products were much higher." This result brings to the fore the importance of *timing* of the OTS when evaluating frequency effects.

The study considered "retention and attraction" effects (equivalent to the REPEAT and CHANGE analyses). It found that the retentive effects, although they existed, were relatively weak except in two categories, but attractive effects were much stronger. Looking in more detail at the latter, the attractive effects described a convex curve close to a straight-line increment with increasing OTS; there was certainly no "threshold" effect at 1 OTS. The same applied when looking at OTS in brand share terms instead of numbers.

Although this study was weakened by the lack of purchase data accurate to the day, it provided a useful confirmation that short-term effects can be observed from panel data.

CENTRAL TV ADLAB

A well-established brand measured on the Central TV Adlab in Britain between late 1985 and mid-1987 showed a strong REPEAT effect. As shown in Table 5.1, the result for this brand was comparable to the findings from the McDonald Study covering nine product categories (which did not include the category of Brand P).

For the other effect measured, CHANGE, the figures for Brand P were unclear, in contrast to the nine-category results from the earlier panel. See Table 5.2.

TABLE 5.1   Brand P; OTS in Interval

	0 %	1 %	2 %	3 %	4 or more %
REPEAT	74	75	79	80	79
cf. McDonald:	54	58	63	67	59

TABLE 5.2   Brand P; OTS in Interval

	0 %	1 %	2 %	3 %	4 or more %
CHANGE	31	34	35	28	31
cf. McDonald:	17	21	27	25	31

Brand P is a single brand, whereas the McDonald figures are several brands and categories combined. For a brand as well established as Brand P, the CHANGE variable may be much less important (note also that the figures in Table 5.2 *exclude* single-brand buyers of P or other brands: they are all "switchers" who bought P *and* other brands). The most likely explanation, taking both measures together, is that because Brand P is already one of the dominant brands in its market, almost the whole job of its advertising is to keep its current buyers buying it, the scope for attracting new or occasional buyers being very small.

Another important finding was the importance of proximity to the purchase. Table 5.3 compares the REPEAT variable with OTS counted from the whole interval, from a 4-day window (i.e., 4 days only before the purchase) and a 2-day window. It is worth noting that this is a product category where more than 50 percent of purchases are made on two days of the week, Friday or Saturday, so that a timing target for OTS delivery makes some sense.

This confirms that when one chances to obtain a concentration of OTS shortly before a purchase, the effects appear to be strengthened. The suggestion is that a very short-term behavioral response is occurring, which may weaken as time lengthens between the OTS and the purchasing occasion.

U.S. Toilet Tissue Data

A study of a small-scale experimental panel in one U.S. market, using data collected during 1984, showed results for toilet tissues (shown in Table 5.4).

The figures in Table 5.4 differ from those quoted earlier in three respects: the OTS are taken from *household,* not individual, TV exposures; the 7-day window ignores whether the last purchase took place within 7 days or not (this may be unimportant for this product category, which tends to be a weekly regular purchase); and single-brand buyers

TABLE 5.3   Brand P: REPEAT Variable

No. of OTS	0	1	2	3	4 or more
	%	%	%	%	%
Whole interval	74	75	79	80	79
4-day window	74	74	75	79	86
2-day window	76	75	78	79	91

TABLE 5.4 U.S. Toilet Tissues: OTS in 7-Day Window

	0 %	1 %	2 or more %
CHANGE	3	9	12
REPEAT	44	36	33
SWITCH	49	52	54

TABLE 5.5 U.S. Toilet Tissues: Three Main Advertised Brands

	Brand A			Brand B			Brand C		
OTS (7-day window)	0	1	2+	0	1	2+	0	1	2+
	%	%	%	%	%	%	%	%	%
CHANGE	10	18	10	16	7	16	8	15	16
REPEAT	37	44	62	44	33	23	40	33	19
SWITCH	42	77	67	51	30	47	56	56	50

as well as switchers are included. The suggestion from the figures is that the advertising was significant in inducing brand switching, but not in retaining loyalty. The sample was too small to break out OTS numbers above 2.

When the three main brands (each accounting for a fifth to a third of the category advertising) were looked at separately, they were found to differ as shown in Table 5.5.

What are we to make of these different patterns? They could perhaps have occurred by chance (and we are dealing with a small sample). But one might have expected a chance pattern to be less extreme. One can easily construct a plausible story to explain what one sees here. It appears that Brand A is successfully using advertising to both attack and consolidate its position, at the expense of Brands B and C. Brand C shows some evidence of occasionally mounting a successful counterattack, with advertising persuading consumers to switch to it (perhaps in conjunction with a deal), but these movements are temporary and soon reversed: the position of A is not permanently dented. External evidence available at the time suggested that this account of the three brands' performance at the time and place in question was generally correct.

There was also evidence that, as the *share* of OTS for Brand A increased, so did the three effectiveness variables, always at the expense of the other two brands. OTS were counted for this analysis in deciles (0–10 percent, 10–20 percent.....90–100 percent). The lowest band (0–10 percent) includes all the intervals when *no* OTS were for the brand (about 4–7 percent of the total).

When the lowest band (0–10 percent OTS share) is compared with the next highest band (11–20 percent OTS share), we find that, for Brand A, the REPEAT variable (the proportion of last-time A buyers who bought it next time) increased by 19 percent: that is, 19 percent *more* A buyers bought A next time when A's share of voice was over 10 percent than when it was under. In contrast, Brands B and C both showed decreases: 14 percent *fewer* B buyers bought B next time when B's share of voice was over 10 percent compared with under, and similarly for C. The CHANGE variable (the proportion switching towards the brand) also went up for Brand A (5 percent) and down for B (–4 percent) with the higher share of voice, but it went *up* for C (by 7 percent), suggesting perhaps that C was attracting some trial but failing to hold buyers.

Table 5.6 below shows these comparisons, and how they change as we move to different levels of share of voice. The first row shows the change, up or down, in REPEAT and CHANGE when SOV above 10 percent is compared with SOV below 10 percent. The second row shows the same comparison when SOV above and below 20 percent are compared, and so on up the scale to 90 percent.

TABLE 5.6   REPEAT and CHANGE

Brands	REPEAT			CHANGE		
	A	B	C	A	B	C
OTS Share above/below	%	%	%	%	%	%
10%	19	–14	–13	5	–4	7
20%	20	–13	–15	5	–4	7
30%	25	–32	–22	10	–5	9
40%	34	–24	–22	5	–6	6
50%	42	–23	–19	7	–5	7
60%	28	–27	–18	8	–6	0
70%	11	–24	–13	9	–4	–3
80%	11	–21	–10	11	–7	–1
90%	11	–21	–6	11	–7	–1

Table 5.6 reinforces the idea that we are perceiving real effects. Brand A's "success" against Brand B, and Brand C's failure to sustain a convincing attack, are shown as related to share of OTS, not just the numbers. It strongly suggests that A's advertising, for whatever reason, was being more effective than B's or C's.

There also was evidence from the same study that advertising may have a short-term effect that increases the closer it is to the purchase occasion. Table 5.7 counts, for the same brands A, B, and C together, the cases where OTS occurred in various "windows" (1-day, 2-day, etc.) before the purchase; all were multibrand buyers. Figures in parentheses show the number of purchase intervals counted in each row.

All the measures show an increasing trend with a shorter "window." All the examples counted above included OTS for the brand, and all deliver a value for SWITCH above 50 percent, increasing the nearer we get in time to the next purchase occasion.

Although this is on a very small scale, it strongly suggests that *shorter* windows do indeed relate to stronger "triggers"; in other words, if advertising is seen in the last day or two before a purchase, the effect for influencing both switching and retention is stronger. If we were to establish this on a proper scale, it would follow not merely that optimum frequency should be aimed for in a short span of days, but that those days should be attached to the day of the week on which most household buying is done, where that can be ascertained.

TABLE 5.7 Number of Cases with OTS in Various "Windows"

Days in "window"	7	6	5	4	3	2	1
O → X (41)	46	39	33	28	27	20	12
X → O (40)	38	30	23	17	13	9	4
X → X (33)	22	20	18	14	11	9	5
O → O (131)	98	78	57	48	42	22	12
	%	%	%	%	%	%	%
CHANGE	32	33	37	37	39	48	50
REPEAT	37	40	44	45	46	50	56
SWITCH	55	57	59	62	57	69	75

THE SCANNER REVOLUTION

When the first edition of this book was published, people were beginning to look to the newly emerging technologies of UPC scanners and peoplemeters to provide the necessary data on a sufficient scale to answer the many remaining questions about effective frequency: in particular, how the effects observed might vary with different brands, OTS timings, media etc. The ARF Key Issues Workshop, held in 1982 to discuss how to take matters forward, included a paper by Gerald Eskin of Information Resources Inc., describing the new Behaviorscan facility.[3]

Unfortunately, until very recently, the promise of these new methods for investigating short-term advertising effects systematically was not realized during the dozen or so years they have been available. A major reason has been the difficulty of obtaining accurate records showing which commercials are transmitted at each second on each TV channel, a difficulty that has not applied in Britain where there are far fewer channels to worry about. As a result, IRI were constrained to rely on split samples where they could control transmissions through cable TV. The findings they have reported relate to a limited set of special cases, in which increased weights or copy changes were tested against controls, and they have not developed the kind of within-individual single-source analysis which was used in the McDonald study.[4]

It is only recently, with the development of electronic on-screen recognition technology, that ways have been found of accurately identifying OTS.

Reichel has reported analysis from Nielsen's Homescan panel over a two-year period. The form of analysis was to look at the shift in brand share following a period of 28 days, comparing those who had or had not been exposed to TV advertising during that period. A total of 45 cases were examined. In 12 of the 45 cases a share increase of 30 percent was found among those exposed to the advertising; 12 others showed an increase of 10–29 percent; 11 increased sales share by 1 to 9 percent; 1 showed no change; and 9 dropped share between 1 and 10 percent. Thus, in nearly four-fifths of the examples, the exposure to advertising was associated with an increase in sales share; the median increase was +10–14 percent.[5]

Reichel also found that the further removed the advertising is from the purchase, the faster the effect drops; 19 brands had advertising budgets substantial enough to make this more sensitive analysis possible. Table

TABLE 5.8   Average Increase in Share

Days since last OTS	Average share change (in month)	Index (1 day = 100)
1	+21.3%	100
2	+17.8%	84
7	+15.1%	71
14	+13.8%	65
28	+10.5%	49

5.8 shows the average increase in share for these 19 brands in homes which made a purchase at different time intervals since last receiving OTS.

Table 5.8 seems to provide a finding that supports Table 5.7 on a much bigger basis. The closer to the purchasing occasion, the higher the response.

STAS (SHORT-TERM ADVERTISING STRENGTH)

The most substantial evidence to date confirming that we can measure short-term effects is provided by John Philip Jones.[6] This is an analysis of 12 product categories from the Nielsen Household Panel of 2,000 homes, covering the whole year of 1991.

The Nielsen Household Panel provides true single-source data, the purchase data stream from a handheld barcode scanner, and the television data stream from peoplemeters. Identification of commercials comes from the Monitor Plus system, which is based on chain of monitoring stations that keep a running log of the advertising appearing at 15-second intervals in the 23 largest Areas of Dominant Influence (ADIs) in the United States. In each region, the information is collected from eight stations: the four broadcast networks, plus the leading cable stations watched in the region. On average, 2.5 million commercials are logged every month.

Jones has developed a measure called STAS, short for Short-Term Advertising Strength. STAS is simply the brand's share of all purchasing occasions. This is compared between those cases where *no* television advertising for the brand had been received by the household during the previous seven days (the BASELINE STAS) and cases where advertising *had* been received (STIMULATED STAS—naturally different amounts of advertising can also be compared.)

STAS is equivalent to Reichel's measure (Table 5.8) and derivable directly from McDonald's REPEAT and CHANGE measures. In fact, it can easily be seen that STAS = REPEAT + CHANGE, added and re-percentaged on the new base of all purchases:

$$\frac{X \to X + O \to X}{X \to X + O \to X + X \to O + O \to O} = \frac{\text{All} \to X}{\text{All purchases}} = \text{STAS}$$

Jones has found that some brands exhibit clear short-term advertising effects, with a STAS differential index above 105 (this is the stimulated STAS indexed on the baseline, no-advertising, STAS). Another group shows no clear directional effect, but the position appears to be holding. A third group, at the bottom, shows a negative effect in the short term: stimulated STAS is actually lower than the baseline. Jones has named these three groups alpha, beta and gamma brands. When "stimulated STAS" are expanded to compare different OTS levels, it is found that alpha brands display a convex curve and gamma brands a reverse, mirror-image convex curve. This is consistent with the explanation of the SWITCH S-shape: advertising for effective, winning brands tends to be seen at the same time as advertising for ineffective, losing brands—and to beat it.

THE EVIDENCE THAT RESPONSE CURVES TEND TO BE CONVEX

Jones makes the important point that what STAS measures is only the *immediate* response to advertising, which is not necessarily lasting. Short-term effects might not persist into medium or longer-term sales increases, although they may do so sometimes. A brand carrying out a successful holding exercise may well exhibit continual short-term effects of this type, which always drop back to the equilibrium position. In the short term, the evidence seems to be that when advertising does work and we have a visible STAS, the response function is convex. The main difference occurs with *one* OTS compared to none; although two or more add some effect, the additional difference is, in relative terms, less. If this principle can be generalized, it supports the view that what most brands have to do is to establish a reasonably continuous presence at not too high a rate, enough to ensure one exposure (leaving aside the need to stand out against competition).

It may be noted that exactly the same strongly convex function, with the largest effect at one OTS, is also shown by the REPEAT and CHANGE fractions in Table 4.5 See Table 5.9.

The evidence from Jones's analysis strongly confirms a growing body of opinion that the "normal" response function for short-term advertising effect is convex, so that the jump from 0 to 1 is the largest effect even if 2 or more push the total even higher. See especially Simon and Arndt, Miles and Arnold and other cases later in this book, plus the discussion in Chapter 9.[7] Jones claims to have found no case, out of the 57 brands he has studied, in which the advertising effect does not follow this pattern (whenever there is an advertising effect at all).

An important consideration is the time interval within which the OTS are clustered before the purchase (or other response measure). In Jones's analysis, a 7-day window was used, and 55% of all cases with any OTS had only 1 OTS. In McDonald's 4-day window, this proportion goes up to over 70%. Clearly, the shorter the period, the more likely that a single OTS will be effective, and the fewer cases there will be of more than 1. Also, someone who receives 1 OTS in 7 days is quite likely to have 4 in a month. So, when comparing different shapes of convex curve, one must not ignore the time-span involved.

This area needs more concentrated study, with particular reference to the effect that the data analyzed and the analysis design may have on the relationships generated. There is certainly not enough information to generalize about the shape and steepness of the convex curve (whether 1, 2 or 3, etc., are the "optimum" number of OTS), even if we agree that the curve is convex. We can do little more with present knowledge than hypothesize under what conditions it might vary (e.g., the strength of the brand, the quality of the advertising, etc.).

TABLE 5.9   OTS in Interval (%)

	0	1	2	3	4+
O → X	12.5	13.3	16.7	14.9	18.0
X → O	12.4	15.1	14.5	13.3	17.1
STAS	27.3	34.5	41.1	42.3	42.8
Increase:		+26	+19	+3	+1

S-SHAPES ARE NOT RULED OUT

The evidence for convex curves as "normal" does not mean that an S-shape or threshold response curve is impossible. But the onus is on those who find one to explain it. Using scanner data to regress indexed sales against television GRPs, Gold finds S-shaped curves for two brands. But (as Jones points out) the threshold occurs at very low levels of advertising delivery in both cases, below 50 GRPs.[8] At such a level, many will see no advertising at all. The two examples shown by Gold are both *almost* convex curves and differ only in the rate of improvement, the level reached, and the point at which the downturn starts. Gold's results, as well as McDonald's, are evidence that the shape of a response curve can be influenced by precisely what is being measured.

More recently, Roberts has reported a study analyzing advertising effects from the AGB Superpanel in Britain.[9] This is single-source data estimated by the "fusion" process, in which purchasing records are aligned with estimated television OTS (for each person) derived from BARB (the UK television industry metered audience measurement vehicle). In this process, actual viewing derived from BARB is ascribed to panel members who have similar viewing and other characteristics. The fusion process "provides each Superpanel housewife with probabilities of viewing commercial breaks at given times. . . . By combining these with the actual spot transmission details for the TV advertising campaign, it is possible to estimate the number of exposures each Superpanel housewife has seen for each week of the campaign."[10]

In his paper Roberts reports 52 weeks, during which a certain brand was relaunched with a heavy TV campaign and a series of follow-up bursts. The variable used was share of brand purchases (similar to STAS). "Those housewives who had seen less than 2 exposures in the four weeks prior to purchasing showed little change in the proportion of their market purchases for the brand. By contrast, housewives who saw 2 or more exposures showed significant increases in their share of brand purchasing. Overall, there was a 19 percent increase in brand share amongst the housewives exposed to advertising—with some evidence that for the most heavily exposed (5 or more exposures within four weeks) the increase was significantly greater."[11] In other words, this appears to be a clear threshold effect, in contrast to Jones's findings.

But, to understand this fully, we would have to know more. The brand was a relaunch, we don't know from what position. And we know nothing about the actual share of the brand, or of its competitors, or what those competitors were doing at the same time in the way of advertising. It is possible that new brands, and those undergoing a relaunch, may have to shout louder to be heard against the competition, unlike the large share brands (Jones's prime examples), which, by the double jeopardy rule, obtain a disproportionate benefit for a lower presence.

The shape of the response curve, for successful advertising, may depend closely (for all we know) on the brand's share and market position. This clearly has important implications for when we should use flighting and high frequency as against continuity at a lower level of OTS.

NOTES

1. Phil Gullen, "Planning Media to Create Sales," *Admap* (October 1985): 505–11. See also Jeremy Elliott, "How Advertising Frequency Affects Advertising Effectiveness: Indications of Change," *Admap* (October 1985): 512–15.

2. Phil Gullen and Hugh Johnson, "Product Purchasing and TV Viewing: Measuring and Relating the Two." ESOMAR: Seminar on New Developments in Media Research, Helsinki, April 9–10, 1986, pp. 345–63.

3. Gerald J. Eskin, "Some New Dimensions in Data Availability." Advertising Research Foundation Conference: "Effective Frequency: The State of the Art," New York, June 4, 1982, pp. 207–28.

4. Information Resources Inc., "How Advertising Works: Management Summary," (Chicago, Illinois, November 1991).

5. Walter Reichel, "New Scanner-Based Analysis System Tracks Sales Results for TV Ad Campaigns," *Marketsense* (Media Dynamics, Inc., May 1992).

6. John P. Jones, *When Ads Work: New Proof That Advertising Triggers Sales* (New York: Lexington Books, 1995).

7. Julian L. Simon and Johan Arndt, "The Shape of the Advertising Response Function," *Journal of Advertising Research,* vol. 20, no. 4 (August 1980): 11–28.

8. Laurence N. Gold, "Let's Heavy Up in St. Louis and See What Happens: Determining TV Effects on Sales through Econometrics." Paper given at the Third Annual ARF Behavioral/Scanner Data Workshop, New York, June 5–6, 1991.

9. Andrew Roberts, "Measuring Advertising Effects through Panel Data." Paper given at 1994 European Advertising Effectiveness Symposium (run by ASI), Brussels, June 9–10, 1994. See also "Media Exposure and Consumer Purchasing: An Improved Data Fusion Technique," paper given at 178th ESOMAR Seminar, 21st March 1994, and "TV Exposure, Brand Buying and Ad Effects," *Admap* (June 1994): 31–37, which quote the same example.

10. Roberts, "Measuring Advertising Effects through Panel Data."

11. Ibid.

CHAPTER 6

OGILVY & MATHER
An Experimental Study of Three Television Dayparts

In 1965, Ogilvy & Mather conducted a carefully controlled experimental study on behalf of four different advertisers, covering eleven brands over eight weeks. As this early effort possessed many of the attributes to be found in later analyses concerned with the frequency issue, an understanding of its methodology will help put into perspective the major features of the other studies discussed in this book. It also was large enough to compare some *media* variables (television dayparts), as well as individual brands.

The Ogilvy & Mather undertaking was before its time and stood alone—but was private and, as such, did not stimulate the industry toward a crystallization on the subject of frequency as did the McDonald study. Its full title was "An Experimental Study of the Relative Effectiveness of Three Television Dayparts"; its objective was to provide better media planning for the efficient use of television through the evaluation of alternative strategies and schedules. The sponsors of the study felt that such questions had previously been answered on an intuitive, judgmental basis, there being no reservoir or backlog of information on these subjects available to media planners. The survey sought to answer three questions:

1. What is the relative effectiveness of advertising in daytime compared with nighttime television?

2. What is the relative effectiveness of advertising in network compared to spot television?

3. How does commercial effectiveness vary with frequency of exposure to the advertising message?

It was felt that since these questions were interrelated, they could all be investigated simultaneously. In the words of its designers, the study was launched:

> . . . To attempt to develop television advertising effectiveness indicators of a type which have not been previously used. It is recognized that such a study must be experimental in nature. As such, it does not purport to be, nor is it presented as, a definitive study supplying eternal truths concerning television advertising effectiveness. Television, being an organic medium, will undoubtedly change over time; and with it, the factors essential to its evaluation and their interrelationships may change. Further, the study demonstrates that there are substantial variations from one brand to another and that generalizations are difficult to make.
>
> Some consistent patterns which lead to generalizations are apparent, however, from the data. This study, we believe, provides the first of a new set of criteria which can contribute significantly to the objectives of the evaluation and selection of television strategies and alternative schedules under consideration.

DESIGN OF THE OGILVY & MATHER STUDY

A number of O&M clients contributed to the support of this test, which made possible a tightly controlled study where results could be measured and more could be learned about how media work. Its design was as follows:

1. The study was structured to measure exposure opportunity to different television schedules for eleven brands of consumer products. The schedules were run over an eight-week period and all activity took place during that time span.

2. Brand preferences were measured for each of the test brands with the same housewife for every week of the eight-week period. This was the criterion measure for the study.

3. The brand preference changes were then related to frequency of exposure to commercials for each of the test brands with the three dayparts involved. This overall approach was accomplished in the following way:

a. A diary panel of housewives was established in the marketing areas where the commercial schedules were run. Each cooperating respondent not only filled out a prequestionnaire, but also kept a diary for each of the eight weeks of the study, and, in addition, completed a post-interview.

b. A key aspect of the diaries was that each respondent recorded her own television viewing for 16 hours a day, seven days a week, by quarter-hour intervals.

c. Primary criterion measurement of brand and preference change was obtained via consumer responses to a constant sum question. This question was in the form of a weekly lottery where the respondent would get a chance to win ten packages of whatever brands she would choose in each of the eleven product categories under study. Since the weekly lottery for each participant represented a significant dollar value, the brand preference measure also provided an incentive for cooperation in the study.

d. Three test areas were used in the study. Across these three areas, special schedules for the eleven participating brands were exposed according to a basic latin square design. This permitted each brand to receive either daytime, nighttime or fringe spot exposure in one of the three test cities. The allocation of the daypart by brand was rotated through the areas so that every area had test television for daytime, nighttime, and fringe spot. The purpose of this approach was to eliminate the influence of test area and brand on the composite results.

e. The schedule to be evaluated for each brand consisted of eight minutes per week in daytime; one minute per week in nighttime; and four minutes per week in fringe spot.

f. To minimize the number of variables involved in interpretation of the results, the same commercial was used for a brand in each of the dayparts throughout the tests, and all commercials were 60-second commercials.

g. Since the broadcast times of each commercial for each brand over the eight-week period were known, it was possible to match the respondent viewing diaries by 15-minute segments to exact "opportunities to see" the commercials. This process, as we have seen, comes as close as possible to actual viewing, and is the method used by all the major advertiser studies to determine exposure.

h. Given schedules of commercials "as sent" by the advertiser, and the record of when respondents were sitting in front of the television set when those exposures occurred, it was possible to determine likely exposure of commercials for each test brand. As in the McDonald study, this means "opportunity to see" and assumes that if the respondent were exposed to the 15-minute segment in which the commercial appeared, she would likely be exposed to the commercial itself.

i. Since a record of commercial "opportunities to see" was thus possible for individual respondents, and since these respondents had given their brand preference change measurements for the eleven brands, the changes for each respondent could then be related to her frequency of exposure to the commercial for each test brand. The analysis made possible by this record of exposures and measurements of consumer preference by brand makes possible daypart comparisons and media planning input not attainable in any other fashion.

j. Each respondent was thus classified as to the number of times she had an opportunity to see a brand's commercial during the eight-week test period.

k. The aggregate brand preference for each exposure group was then computed for the period immediately prior to the start of the test and for the average of the eight test weeks. The average of all eight test weeks was used, in order to include in the measurement the total effect of the advertising. A percentage change in the brand preference, with the prepreference as a base, was then computed for each exposure group.

l. The basis for the analysis, therefore, was a frequency distribution of the respondent audience for a brand advertising over the eight weeks, from which brand preference changes among different exposure groups could be determined. In this way it was possible to examine the effect of frequency of exposure, and the aim of the study was fulfilled because shifts in brand preference could be related directly to TV viewing activity.

A distinct advantage of the Ogilvy & Mather analysis, as of most of the other proprietary studies discussed here, is that they encompass a number of different brands and schedules, thereby affording the opportunity to draw generalizations from a review of the total experience of all test brands. In the O&M study, for example, all the computations that led to the results presented here are based on three typical schedules—daytime, nighttime, and fringe spot—that can be purchased with equal expenditures of funds.

RESULTS OF THE STUDY

On the subject of frequency effectiveness, the Ogilvy & Mather study led to the following conclusions:

1. *There is a direct relationship between brand preference change and frequency of exposure.* As a result, the frequency of exposure that a television schedule on each of the three dayparts affords to the reach of that schedule is critical in evaluating its effectiveness.

2. The importance of frequency is pointed up by the fact that, at the one-exposure level, all three dayparts have only a nominal effect and all are virtually equal.

3. As frequency of exposure increases, however, substantial differences appear in the relationship between exposure and brand preference changes for the three dayparts.

4. Below the level of four exposures, the effect of nighttime network on brand preference change is less than the effect of either daytime or fringe spot within that same range.

5. When frequency of exposure in nighttime network reaches a level of six or more, viewer reaction to the advertising becomes more

positive than it does with groups similarly exposed in fringe spot or daytime.

6. In either case, it is apparent that consideration of the reach—*and particularly the frequency distribution of that reach afforded by a given schedule*—is the key to evaluating a schedule (i.e., in comparison to alternative schedules).

7. As Figure 6.1 shows, frequency for all dayparts increased more or less constantly (even up to 20 exposures over an eight-week period) without a decline. Frequency clearly produces results, although those results can differ by time of day within the television environment.

FIGURE 6.1 Index of Brand Preference Change Induced by Frequency of Exposure in Three Television Dayparts (11 Brand Composite)

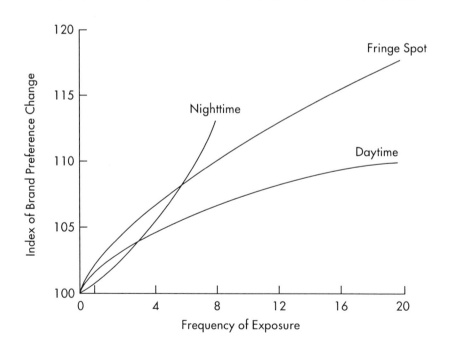

8. Figure 6.2 shows, for three product groups, how receipt of advertising affected brand preference change, compared to when there was zero OTS (as represented by the vertical line). Fringe spot worked best for food products; daytime for household products, and nighttime for toiletry products.

9. Figure 6.3 illustrates that frequency-of-exposure effects can also differ dramatically by brand.

Overall, then, the Ogilvy & Mather study provided strong evidence that frequency of exposure produces positive results, but is subject to wide differences in effectiveness, not only by dayparts, but also by categories of products and brands within these. Its authors concluded that they had

FIGURE 6.2 Comparison of Brand Preference Change by Product Category (Three Television Dayparts)

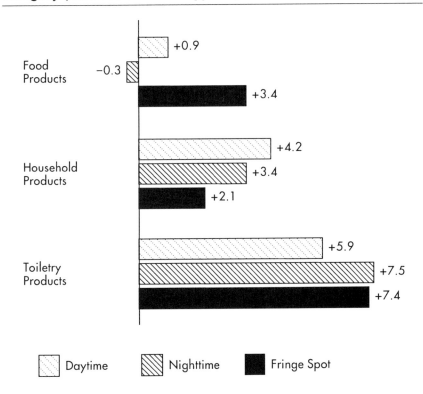

FIGURE 6.3 Brand Preference Change Induced by Frequency of Exposure to Daytime Television (Food Products)

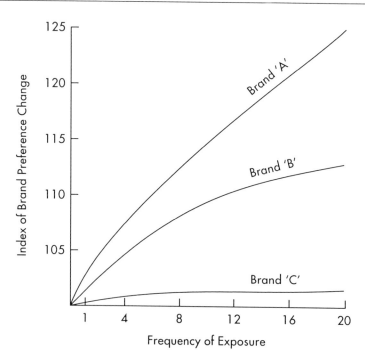

made progress toward a workable system for quantifying television schedule evaluations, which, previous to their efforts, had been made on a judgmental and subjective basis. They had shown clearly that the effect of one exposure was no more than nominal for any daypart, and that frequency effectiveness inputs were a key factor in choosing among media planning alternatives. Moreover, they had found that, although effectiveness increases with frequency, it usually does so at a steady, but generally decreasing, rate: a convex response curve.

CHAPTER 7

MAJOR ADVERTISER ADTEL SCHEDULING STUDY

Another significant major effective-frequency study, carried out after the McDonald and Ogilvy & Mather projects, was conducted by one of the hundred largest advertisers. This study, completed in 1975, employed as a measurement criterion diary-recorded purchasing within an AdTel split-cable (CATV) television market. It measured sales response relative to different exposure frequencies within the framework of the usual media scheduling practices of the brands involved.

BACKGROUND OF ADTEL CABLE TELEVISION SYSTEM

AdTel grew out of a feasibility study conducted by the Advertising Research Foundation, showing which areas best met the demographic, legal, and economic requirements for such a system. A market was chosen that had:

- A television set–owning population in excess of 35,000 households and 100,000 people,

- Reasonable typicality in terms of demographics, cultural and economic patterns, television viewing habits, and retail shopping facilities,

- A new CATV system, where both cables could be installed simultaneously,

• One, and only one, affiliate of each of the three television networks carried on the CATV system.

DESIGN OF THE STUDY

By 1974 the whole question of effective frequency was fast becoming a burning issue for the advertising industry. Since the AdTel facility was well suited to tightly controlled experimentation, their people perceived the issue as a timely project and sought to construct a definitive study of frequency effects. They worked to make advertising and viewing data for AdTel households available, along with purchase data from AdTel panels, and sought to interest advertisers in participating in their program.

The main participant in the undertaking described here conducted several different brand studies—one in each of a number of different product categories. The design of the approach for each brand and product category is shown in Table 7.1.

Starting in September 1974, nine months of family purchase data were obtained for five brands and categories. The brands involved are identified by their budget levels and mean share of advertising in their categories, as shown in Table 7.2.

TABLE 7.1   Timing of the AdTel Study of Brand Analysis

Purchasing behavior	28 weeks	28 weeks
Viewing behavior		28 weeks
	March '74 Sep '74	April '75

TABLE 7.2   Budget Level and Mean Share of Advertising

Brand	Approximate National Advertising Rate	Mean Share of Category Advertising
A	$8.2MM	58%
B	$2.1MM	72%
C	$7.6MM	15%
D	$5.1MM	61%
E	$4.7MM	42%

In addition to the purchase information, viewing data were obtained for two-week periods in November, February and July, and projected for each family for the entire test period. By placing the media schedule of the advertiser's brands against the projected viewing, it was possible to estimate the probable exposures per household. All competitive advertising in the market was monitored and, when compared to household viewing, it was also possible to *estimate probable competitive exposures per household.* This was a unique and important capability of the AdTel studies.

All of the data were organized by four-week purchase periods; the overall results reflect an average of the four-week periods throughout the test. A key part of the analysis involved determining exposure and share-of-advertising effects in retaining users and in attracting users. For this purpose, prior use was defined as being use within the 12-week period prior to each four-week period during the test; in other words, there was a rolling definition of users rather than a static one.

The advertiser's approach in relating household purchases to exposure to its own and competitive brand advertising might best be described as one that utilized a series of successive approximations (formulas) to obtain the best fit. At each state, a number of variables and relationships were hypothesized; e.g., that additional exposures increased the probability of buying the brand, but at a diminishing rate. A computer program (step-wise multiple regression) then allowed one variable at a time into the equation if, and only if, it improved the household-by-household buying predictions.

After the results of each run were examined, new hypotheses were created and the data were re-run. It was felt that the end equation derived through this process supplied the truest estimates for significant variables related to the prediction of household purchases. Graphically, the data— by exposure frequency for the average four-week period by each brand— are shown, starting with Figure 7.1, after the following technical description of the approach used in this study.

TECHNICAL DESCRIPTION

Step-wise regression analysis was used to predict household purchase in each of the four-week periods. (The first period was excluded so that whether or not there was a purchase in the previous period it could be used as a covariate control.) The dependent variable was simply whether or not at least one purchase was made in a given four-week period.

The independent variables were: number of exposures, share of exposures, whether there had been any exposure or none, and various derivations of these. There were also a number of covariate controls according to whether or not the brand had been purchased in the previous period, or several previous periods, and the interaction of these factors with non-commercial exposure to cable television; a further range of independent variables was created by multiplying each independent variable by each covariate control. These independent variables and controls were selected only after considerable trial and error.

A range of possible response functions was hypothesized, including a linear function with increasing exposures, a convex growth function with increasing exposures, a step function (exposed/not exposed), and growth functions with exposure numbers differentiated according to the *share* of exposures.

RESULTS OF THE STUDY

Figures 7.1 to 7.5 display the results for five brands. All the regressions shown were highly significant.

FIGURE 7.1   Brand E

Findings for this brand were somewhat different than for the others:

1. For user households, there was a sharp initial increase in buying probability at one exposure, with the effect of additional exposures diminishing very rapidly.

2. For user households, the initial advertising effects were greater with the shares of advertising (i.e., less competition), but the effects of additional exposures were very small at all share-of-advertising levels.

3. For non-users, there were no differences related to different shares of competitive advertising.

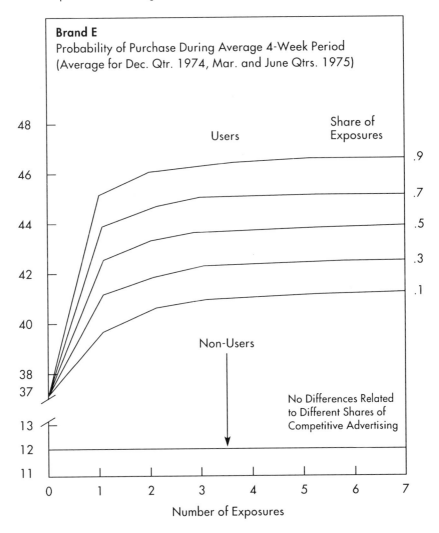

Brand E
Probability of Purchase During Average 4-Week Period
(Average for Dec. Qtr. 1974, Mar. and June Qtrs. 1975)

FIGURE 7.2 Brand C

1. Both user and non-user households showed small but steadily increasing probabilities of buying with additional advertising exposures.

2. Both user and non-user households showed stronger exposure effects at higher shares of category advertising.

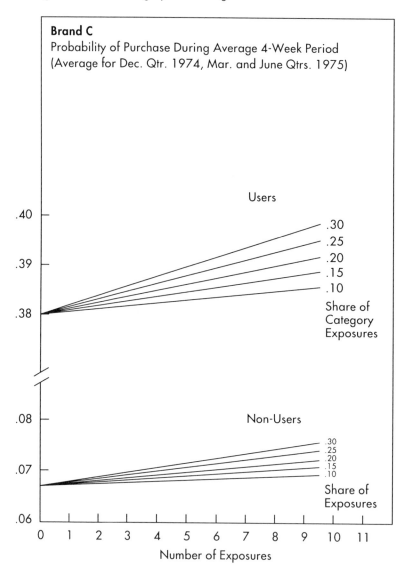

Brand C
Probability of Purchase During Average 4-Week Period
(Average for Dec. Qtr. 1974, Mar. and June Qtrs. 1975)

FIGURE 7.3 Brand D

Findings for this brand, which tested two different media plans, were as follows:

1. For user households, there were sharply increasing probabilities of buying with additional exposures, in both plans tested.
2. For user households, the probabilities of buying at each level of exposure were higher with Plan II.
3. For users and for non-users, share of advertising did not appear to affect the value of different number of exposures.

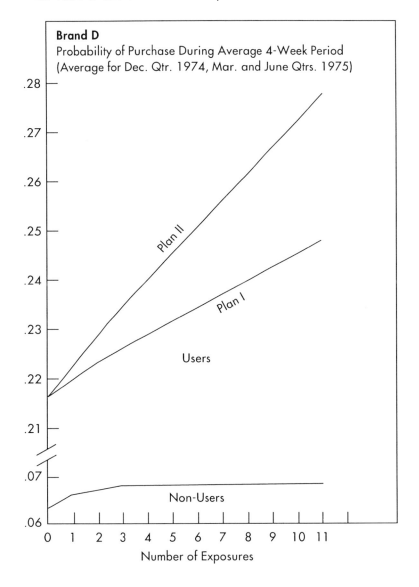

Brand D
Probability of Purchase During Average 4-Week Period
(Average for Dec. Qtr. 1974, Mar. and June Qtrs. 1975)

FIGURE 7.4   Brand A

Both user and non-user households showed increases with exposure, but non-users did not increase in buying probability with additional exposures.

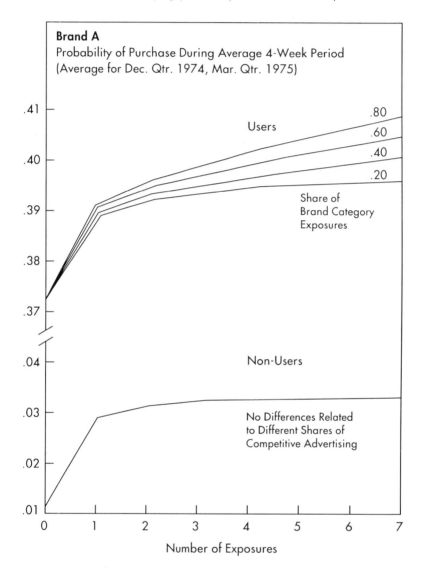

FIGURE 7.5   Brand B

Two plans were tested, as with Brand D. Results were very similar to those for Brand D:

1. For user households, there were sharply increasing probabilities of buying with additional exposures, in both plans tested.
2. For user households, the probabilities of buying at each level of exposure were higher with Plan II.
3. For users and for non-users, share of advertising did not appear to affect the value of different numbers of exposures.

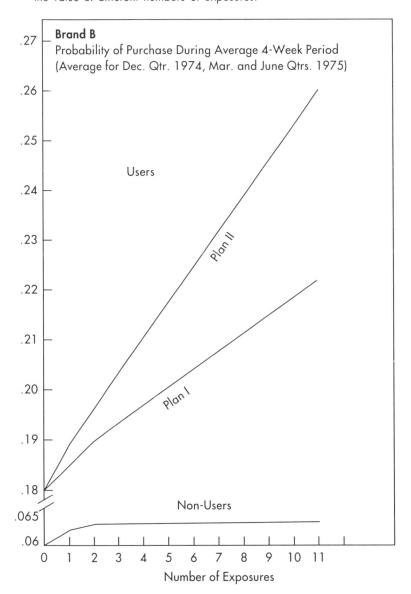

Brand B
Probability of Purchase During Average 4-Week Period
(Average for Dec. Qtr. 1974, Mar. and June Qtrs. 1975)

CONCLUSIONS

This advertiser drew the following general conclusions from his five
brand analyses:

1. There are different probabilities of buying associated with different
   household exposure levels:

   • User households show a sharp initial growth and a further steady
     increase in the probability of buying, with additional advertising
     exposures.

   • User households show the best increases in probability of buying
     when additional exposures and a greater share of category ad-
     vertising exist together.

   • Non-user households show an initial increase but very little
     growth in probability of buying, with additional advertising
     exposures.

2. The largest values for additional exposures were noted for Brand
   B and Brand D users. *These brands had the highest share of
   advertising in their categories.* They were also different from the
   other brands on the basis of having a lower probability that a user
   in the preceding quarter would buy again within an average four-
   week period without any exposure to advertising. This repeat-
   purchase probability was estimated at 18 percent for Brand B and
   22 percent for Brand D, compared to 37 percent for Brand A, 38
   percent for Brand C and 37 percent for Brand E.

   Lower repeat-purchase probabilities of this kind (in each of the
   four-week periods measured) could be due to lower brand loyalty,
   smaller promotion budgets or longer purchase cycles. Of these
   possibilities, the longer purchase cycle might best account for the
   differences between Brands B and D, and Brands A, C, and E. If
   this is true, we might then generalize that brands with longer purchase cycles are likely to benefit most from higher frequencies of
   exposure.

   The media planning implications for brands such as B and D
   might include a greater use of daytime advertising, where the same
   dollars would purchase greater frequency of exposure. It is also
   possible that daytime advertising for such brands should attempt to
   have continuity on a limited number of programs during a given

time period, instead of being scattered over many programs. Still another possibility might be smaller space/time units, to increase frequency while maintaining reach.

3. Share-of-advertising effects appeared to be greater for Brands E, A and C—in that order—and non-existent for the other two brands. (The mean shares of advertising for the advertiser's brands in the categories as they defined them were: E–42%, C–15%, B–72%, D–61%, and A–58%.)

   Although there is no readily apparent explanation why the above brands would benefit most by increasing their shares of advertising, there are some media implications for brands responding in this way. It would seem that such brands should seek to dominate whatever medium they choose to be in. Which is to say that, while not looking for high frequency of exposure within a medium, they might do well to seek out media not being used by competition and spend the funds generated from lowering the frequency in their primary medium.

The findings in this major advertiser AdTel study are somewhat different from those reported earlier in this book. It can be partly attributed to the difference in sizes of brands involved in the study, as well as to other aspects of the analytical approach. A number of observations ought to be made in this regard:

1. The AdTel study was different by virtue of its separate analysis of users and non-users. Considering the commanding shares of advertising held by these brands in their categories, it is not surprising that separate user/non-user analyses were involved. Most of the brands obviously possessed a large share, and so had the primary objective of retaining and motivating users, as opposed to attracting non-users or potential switchers.

   This is an important distinction, for it is quite likely that these large brands would not necessarily lose to a competitor on one "opportunity to see." In effect, such large brands did not have the problem of falling below competitive share of voice.

2. Brands A, B, D, and E were obviously the large brands, judging by their shares of advertising in each category. Their responses for one "opportunity to see" in a four-week period differed from that of

Brand C, a minor share-of-advertising brand more typical of the average brand in most categories. For a brand such as C, marginal one-exposure responses are observed. Hence it is obvious that the very large brands involved in this study behave differently from the normal brand in perhaps more competitive categories.

3. The Ogilvy & Mather study did not specifically break out users, but the samples for the studies contained users in proportion to the market share of the various brands. If a similar figure were reported from the AdTel scheduling study—i.e., if a weighted user/nonuser number were provided—it would lessen the size of the increase for one OTS, and the effects would show up more in line with those of the other studies. A similar difference between large and small-share brands is evident from Jones's STAS findings.

4. The AdTel scheduling study does generally agree with the others in terms of the growth of response at the two-exposure level and beyond.

5. Also, for as many as 10 or 11 exposures in four weeks, the AdTel study showed no evidence of decay for any of the brands (although some did plateau after only a few exposures), which is consistent with the previous studies.

6. Differences in potential sales by different media plans (Plan I and Plan II, in several cases) indicate the leverage of each plan when different frequency patterns are employed against consumers.

CHAPTER 8

PRINT ADVERTISING

Television has dominated the effective frequency debate, and all the studies discussed so far have been wholly or mainly concerned with it. This is not surprising. With television, the concept of multiple opportunities to see within a relatively short time span (say, a four-week schedule), seems to make obvious sense; moreover, it can be predicted easily from the viewing pattern. Someone viewing a program will have commercials in that program put before him willy-nilly; the heavier his viewing, the more his OTS. A magazine issue, on the other hand, can take a relatively long time to achieve its full reach, and frequency seems to be more in the control of the reader; repeated exposures can be avoided simply by turning the page—no one has to look at the same insertion twice. The idea of effective frequency seems harder to pin down in print.

Nowadays, we might wish to quarrel with this simplified distinction; we might argue, for example, that television viewers are not so passive and helpless as all that. But the thought has certainly been there. The 1979 edition of this book mostly ignored print, because little was then available to be quoted.

NEW STUDIES ON PRINT

More recently, a number of studies have been done specifically involving print, and it is appropriate to devote a chapter to these.

BOGART, TOLLEY, AND ORENSTEIN: PRINT ADS CAN STIMULATE SHORT-TERM BUYING

An important early study was described by Bogart et al. in the *Journal of Advertising Research.*[1] Although strictly it did not cover frequency (except in the sense of 0 or 1), it did provide sound experimental evidence that print advertising can stimulate an immediate response observable in purchasing terms.

The experiment was set up with considerable care. Matched samples of newspaper delivery routes were selected in six cities. For two successive days, morning newspapers were delivered to those homes containing test pages that had been inserted after the copies came off the press. These test pages were produced so as to be indistinguishable from the rest of the paper. On each day, there were two sets of test pages, each containing a different selection of advertisements, which were delivered to the two matched groups; thus, each sample was a "control" for the other. Interviews were carried out with the housewives on the evening of the day following the newspaper delivery; thus, for each test ad, about one and one-half days were allowed between the OTS and the interviewing. About 100 housewives were interviewed in each city in respect of each test ad: across all six cities, therefore, there were 600 interviews for each ad, and 600 controls.

The important finding of the study was that, in the one and a half days since the OTS, taking all the brands and ads together, 14 percent more purchases of the advertised brand took place among the test group than among the control group, a difference that "could occur by chance only once in eight times"; there was also a 10 percent greater brand share, 15 percent more sales of any brand of the advertised product for the six cases where this comparison could be made, and 4 percent more first choices of the advertised brand for purchase "next time," all highly significant differences. Within these average effects, there was evidence of considerable differences in the effectiveness of individual ads, and almost no relationship between the sales effects and whether the ad was recalled or recognized. The authors concluded:

It is apparent that an ad may arouse widespread attention and high readership without persuading the few people in the immediate market who are ready to buy. Conversely, an ad may rank low in its appeal to the general reader and still have a strong sales effect upon the very few prospective customers in the immediate market.[2]

Even though it can tell us nothing about frequency effects, this study was valuable for the evident care taken to produce high-quality test material (no mean task in this field), and to control the test and rule out any spurious effects. As a result, it provides clear evidence of print advertising being able to affect purchasing in the very short term, as we have found for television, among "those who are in the market at the time" (usually, a small minority). This last is also an important point when we are thinking about frequency.

THE TIME–SEAGRAM STUDY: EVIDENCE FOR FREQUENCY EFFECTS

Bogart and his colleagues demonstrated, among other things, that it is difficult to study differential advertising effects convincingly in print without considerable help and investment from the publisher. This was shown even more forcefully by the next major study to appear, the Time–Seagram project. This study was designed specifically to demonstrate frequency effects, if they existed. It involved a large-scale and protracted collaboration between an advertiser, Joseph E. Seagram & Sons, and a magazine publisher, Time Inc.[3]

Two markets were chosen: Missouri (state) and Milwaukee (city). Eight Seagram brands were to be used in the test. The markets had to meet the following criteria:

- No other advertising was scheduled for the eight brands during the test year.
- There was reasonable distribution of the brands.
- For production control, marketing had to be handled out of the same printing plant (Chicago) for both magazines used.

The study ran for over 48 weeks, among subscribers to two magazines, *Time* and *Sports Illustrated*. It was so organized that each subscriber would receive:

2 brands: 0 ads each month: overall dosage 0
2 brands: 1 ad each month: overall dosage 12
2 brands: 2 ads each month: overall dosage 24
2 brands: 4 ads each month: overall dosage 48

This design was balanced so that each group of subscribers received these dosage levels for different sets of brands, and every care was taken to avoid bias (including rotation of the ads so that they appeared an equal number of times at the front and back of the magazine and on left and right pages).

Data were collected by weekly mailed questionnaires, on awareness and claimed purchase. Each week, different people were mailed; no one was questioned more than once. The interest is therefore to see how the different dosage levels (pooled across brands) differ in the speed at which awareness, etc., is gained as the different frequencies of OTS build up throughout the test.

The results showed that there were sharp increases in the first week or so of the campaign, followed by less steep but continuing rises as the test progressed to 48 weeks. This applied at each dosage level, but was progressively higher (both a higher starting point and a steeper rise) with each higher dosage. This applied to four of the measures: brand awareness, advertising awareness, favorable brand ratings, and "willingness to buy." This all looks like good evidence of increased frequency creating an improved impact (remember, no other advertising was going on). There is no clear explanation of special gains produced by the first insertion; one hypothesis (unproven) is that those people who are most susceptible to advertising tend to notice the insertions early, while the less easily influenced take longer to do so.

In all these four measures, there was one difference between the four "high awareness" brands (average awareness 66 percent with 0 dosage) and the four "low awareness" brands (average awareness 25 percent 0 dosage). The high awareness brands have less room to increase: they show initially a U-shaped pattern, rising sharply after the first week, dropping back a little, and then, after a few weeks, resuming the rise, which then continues to the end of the test. The low awareness brands start more slowly and describe a smoother, diminishing-returns curve, without the initial fall-back; also, from their lowest starting point, they can increase much more (for example, the high dosage, low awareness brands doubled in brand awareness, whereas the high dosage, high awareness brands could only rise 10 percent).

All brands were purchased at a low level. But compared with 0 dosage, the different levels showed gains in claimed purchases as follows:

Dosage	Usage (%)	Purchase (%)
1/month	43.0	110.8
2/month	43.4	113.5
4/month	72.3	170.3

From this it seems that purchase gains were much larger than gains in usage, and that for both measures the highest dosage level, 4 per month, was much more effective than the other two.

If we say that this study shows greater results from increased frequency, what kind of "frequency" are we talking about? There is no implication of OTS being tightly clustered in time. Even the heavyweight dosage of four ads per month implies a rate of only *one* OTS per week, substantially less than the frequencies we have been considering in television.

The Time–Seagram study is important evidence that magazine advertising "works," and that its effects can be proportionate to the number of insertions or OTS delivered. But it does not show that two, three or more OTS have a greater probability of being *quickly followed* by a purchase than only one. The results are consistent with a different interpretation: that any single insertion, seen once, can be followed by a "lift" in awareness and propensity to purchase, that subsequent insertions increase that lift (with diminishing returns, a convex response function) and that the different slopes of these curves are the result of different rates of repetition.

At the end of Chapter 3, a distinction was drawn between the effect of frequency clusters in television (Krugman, McDonald) and the very different measurement in the Zielske experiment, and it was suggested that this would be better referred to by a different name than "frequency" (possibly "repeat-rate"). The Time–Seagram study is a Zielske-type experiment, not a Krugman/McDonald one: Comparisons are made using measurements at regular intervals between groups to insertions at regular but different repeat rates. It is instructive to compare the response curves charted in Time–Seagram with Zielske's curves—they are very similar.

THE *FAMILY CIRCLE* STUDY OF PRINT ADVERTISING EFFECTIVENESS

A more recently reported project, involving the magazine *Family Circle,* makes a point similar to the Time–Seagram study.[4] This study used the Citicorp POS database, which continuously scans supermarket purchases made by participating households: with over 300,000 households researched, it is "by far the largest panel in the United States." The test ran over 28 weeks: a 12-week base period, 4 weeks during which advertisements appeared in the magazine, and a further 12-week "post" period. In the three markets where the test took place, the panel was divided into two matched groups: one which purchased *Family Circle* (in store or on subscription), and a control which was "not known to have purchased the issue." Although other media were not controlled, there was good evidence that *Family Circle* readership was more or less unrelated to television viewing weight, but correlated strongly with readership of other magazines.

A total of 22 brands were measured. They ran one or more four-color pages in the issue, had reliable data available on purchase and distribution, and had at least 70 percent of their category sales through supermarkets and grocery stores.

Sales increased for 15 of the 22 brands from the base to the test period, in the test sample compared to the control. The average increase was just under 20 percentage points. There was also evidence of category sales expansion, and of sales effects persisting after the test. For one brand described in detail, Nabisco Harvest Crisps, households that had purchased the *Family Circle* issue bought 19.8 percent more than the control in the base period, 50.8 percent more in the test period, and 43 percent more in the period that followed.

The study was not designed to produce direct evidence on frequency. However, it could be assumed from known purchasing patterns that the test sample (of purchasers and subscribers) were much more likely to have seen other issues than the control sample. The following compares the cumulative sales differences over the whole period, test over control, for brands that had one, two, three, or four insertions during the relevant period, the first half of 1990.

Frequency (insertions)	Number (brands)	Cumulative sales difference (%)
1	5	12
2	8	26
3	7	33
4	2	7

The two ads with four insertions were not for specific products, but categories (e.g., National Dairy Board's ad for cream cheese): a 7 percent rise in this case was felt to be creditable. All the others were for specific and distinct brands.

Like the Time–Seagram study, this is evidence that repeated insertions in a magazine can have quite a strong incremental effect on sales. Like Time–Seagram also, it is a repeat-rate (Zielske-type) study rather than a "frequency" one, even though only one measurement is taken to compare the different exposure groups (before–after the four-week insertion period). It is easier to read the evidence as suggesting a series of Zielske-type curves, rising at different (weekly) rates, than as a higher purchase probability following two or three OTS rather than one.

ZIFF–DAVIS: A CLUSTERED OTS "FREQUENCY"

Paul Chook reports a study that artificially created the possibility of receiving more than one exposure from the same issue. It thus avoided the dilemma discussed above of how to interpret "frequency" effects from insertions in successive issues. If a single issue containing two or three insertions produces a better result than an issue containing only one, it is fair to suppose that we are seeing a genuine frequency effect on probability of purchase. Because this study deliberately reproduced a clustering of OTS within the same time frame, it is closer to a TV (McDonald) scenario than what is usual with print.[5]

Three tests were done, in 1978, 1982, and 1983, using in each case an issue of a different Ziff–Davis (later CBS) "special interest" title. They were in order: *Stereo Review, Flying* and *Boating*. Each test was done in three markets: Boston, Washington, D.C., and Dallas/Fort Worth. In each market, three matched samples of subscribers to the magazine were selected, each receiving a different advertising treatment.

Each issue contained six advertisements appropriate to the interest group subscribing to the magazine: three were "general" ads (i.e., for products that might have been advertised to the same readership anywhere), the other three "generic" ads (i.e., products that fit in with the magazine's subject matter, such as hi-fi equipment in *Stereo Review*, yachts, and marine equipment in *Boating*, etc.). Each advertisement was given a different treatment for each subscriber group: one group received an issue containing no ad; another group, 1 ad; and the third group, 3 ads, according to the following design:

		Subscriber Samples		
		No. 1	No. 2	No. 3
General ads				
	A	0	1	3
	B	1	3	0
	C	3	0	1
Generic ads				
	X	0	1	3
	Y	1	3	0
	Z	3	0	1

The 3-insertion treatment has simulated multiple opportunities-to-see. The same advertising execution was used each time, and the insertions appeared in the front, middle and back of the issue. Single-issue insertions were rotated so that each insertion appeared equally in each issue position.

Subscribers were telephoned in advance and asked to look through each issue, opening every page. Thus the test approximated forced exposure as closely as possible. Interviews were done, ideally 24 hours after receipt of the issue, but in practice with a longer time interval (average two days).

The key questions asked were advertising recall, verified ad recall (respondent proves he has seen the ad by playing back visual or copy points), brand awareness ("top three brands that come to mind") and brand salience ("brand that comes to mind first"). All these measures tended to increase with 1 insertion compared with 0, and with 3 insertions compared with 1, although the extent of the lift varied considerably between the ads, as did the level of false claiming (when 0 advertising was seen). The average results were:

	No. of Insertions			Lift (over 0)	
	0 %	1 %	3 %	with 1 %	with 3 %
Claimed ad recall					
General	6	19	37	13	31
Generic	11	25	44	14	33
Verified recall					
General	1	12	27	11	26
Generic	3	15	29	12	26
Brand awareness					
General	30	33	39	3	9
Generic	13	18	23	5	10
Brand salience					
General	13	15	18	2	5
Generic	6	8	12	2	6

These were respectable results, even if we think they may have been somewhat heightened by the way the test design ensured likelihood of exposure. They are evidence that there can be frequency effects, at least on intermediate variables, if a number of OTS are delivered close together—more likely to be achieved in the real world by insertions in different magazines than by multiple insertions in one issue. The drawback is that it was not possible to measure actual purchase probabilities.

BUSINESS-TO-BUSINESS ADVERTISING: THE ARF/ABP STUDY

Most evidence about frequency effects comes inevitably from frequently purchased consumer goods for the obvious reason: time-lags are short, and the data can be built up quickly. It is rare to find an experiment designed to look for advertising frequency effects on business or industrial purchases with much longer purchase decision cycles.

The Advertising Research Foundation and the Association of Business Publishers reported the results of their joint experiment in 1987.[6] It was very carefully constructed. Four products were selected (from a number of manufacturers who wanted to take part) which were relatively new, with reasonable decision cycles, advertised only in controlled circulation trade magazines and with good sales data available (participant manufacturers were asked to avoid other promotion during the test year). For three of the products, three matched samples of end users, who also subscribed to the magazines, were chosen; each of these samples were given respectively a "high," "medium," and "low" advertising treatment, defined in terms of the number and rate of advertising insertions during the year. For the fourth product, there were nine treatment cells, to take account of dealer as well as end-user advertising. Several variables were monitored during the test: product awareness, ad recall, manufacturer's name recall, sales inquiries, sales, and profit.

Frequency can be seen to have a different meaning in this context. In the Time–Seagram and *Family Circle* examples, repeated insertions in successive issues over a period may be seen as a series of singletons, as we have seen, each of which could be followed by a purchase opportunity, rather than a genuine multiple-exposure "frequency." In other words, we may simply be looking at one OTS tending to have an effect compared to 0 OTS, and the effect increasing over time with the increasing number of ones. This is not really "frequency," if by that we mean that a purchase is more probable after two or three OTS. But in the business–industrial context, where purchases are occasional, discretionary, and serious (two out of the three products were expensive), a build-up of successive insertions over a year may really be "frequency" in the precise sense, because there is not a repeat purchase opportunity every month or so. This all goes to show how very careful we have to be in comparing different studies together in order to draw common conclusions.

If we can agree to accept the high, medium and low advertising cells as different "frequencies" in the precise sense, a number of effects were shown relating to frequency. In particular, there were effects on the most important variables: sales enquiries, sales, and profits. The results cannot be summarized easily, and it is best to refer to the full paper.

MILLWARD BROWN

In recent years, the research agency Millward Brown has been publishing findings that differentiate print advertising from television, which are relevant to the question of what "frequency" can mean in a magazine context.

In a 1992 paper, Gordon Brown made the point that exposure to magazine advertising is "often very delayed indeed," as opposed to television advertising, where "most exposures occur when it is transmitted or soon after."[7] In a large-scale study in 1990, they found that half the total exposures to an issue of a typical quality monthly magazine "have still to occur 8 or 9 weeks after the publication date. And 15 percent of the exposures occur more than 20 weeks after publication date." This fact must underlie the rising repeat-rate effects found in Times–Seagram and the other studies above: theoretically, all the OTS occur together, during the publication interval of the issue, but *actually* a large proportion of these OTS occur much later, and take longer to build up.

But there is evidence from another study in 1991, known as "Magtrack," that print exposures apparently generate much higher levels of advertising awareness than television exposures do (on average, nearly three times as much), and that, unlike television, those effects are immediate, from one exposure. Successive exposures to the same ad produce rapidly declining response. Brown argues that these findings relate to a quite different "psychology" attached to television compared to print. Whereas television is essentially passive, print ads are screened out if not interesting and actively processed if they are—and, processed once, they do not need to be again.

The implication for frequency, applied to print, appears to be that one should look for a "repeat-rate" of insertions calculated to deliver OTS (building up gradually over time) sufficient to produce exposures which will cover the interested market, one exposure generally being enough to each execution.

NOTES

1. L. Bogart, B.S. Tolley, and F. Orenstein, "What One Little Ad Can Do," *Journal of Advertising Research,* vol. 10, no. 4 (August 1970): 3–13.

2. Bogart et al., "What One Little Ad Can Do," p. 13.

3. "A Study of the Effectiveness of Advertising Frequency in Magazines: The Relationship between Magazine Advertising Frequency and Brand Awareness, Advertising Recall, Favorable Brand Rating, Willingness to Buy and Product Use and Purchase." Time Incorporated in Association with Joseph E. Seagram & Sons, Inc., published by Time Incorporated, New York, 1982.

4. R. McPheters, "Use of Scanner Data to Measure the Effects of Magazine Advertising and Frequency on Product Volume." ESOMAR Conference, Tokyo, July 1992.

5. P.H. Chook, "A Continuing Study of Magazine Environment, Frequency, and Advertising Performance," *Journal of Advertising Research,* vol. 25, no. 4 (August/September 1985): 23–33.

6. "The Impact of Business Publication Advertising on Sales and Profits: A Joint Project of the Advertising Research Foundation and the Association of Business Publishers." New York, 1987.

7. Gordon Brown, "TV and Print Advertising." Paper given at ARF Electronic Media & Research Technologies Workshop, New York, Dec. 1–2, 1992. See also: Gordon Pincott, "An Examination of Wear-out and Exposure Over Time," Millward Brown International, June 1993; and Gordon Brown, "The Awareness Problem: Attention and Memory Effects from TV and Magazine Advertising," *Admap* (January 1994): 15–20.

CHAPTER 9

WHAT ARE WE NOW IN A POSITION TO CONCLUDE?

The first edition of this book ended with a chapter headed "Conclusions," in which 12 hypotheses were put forward, more or less tentatively, based on the evidence reviewed. Now, more than a decade later, with some new information and much debate and introspection under our belts, we must attempt again to summarize what we know, or think we know.

Conclusion 1: There is convincing evidence that advertising, when it is good enough to work at all, may have short-term effects, including effects of purchase probability.

This is a broader statement, and may well seem less instantly satisfying, than the first conclusion offered in the first edition. The reason is that there is now substantial evidence (e.g., Simon and Arndt, Miles and Arnold, Jones, among others[1]) that the *convex curve* is the commonest shape for a response function rather than the threshold (S-shaped) curve. This opens the possibility that a single exposure or OTS can be effective in at least a number of common marketing situations, even if two or three are more effective still.

The first edition offered as its first conclusion that:

One exposure of an advertisement to a target group consumer within a purchase cycle has little or no effect in all but a minority of circumstances. . . . On this finding there was general agreement among all the studies covered . . . there is little question that a single exposure provides no more than a nominal advertising effect.

Now, we must say this is far from obvious. Simon and Arndt[2] have collected evidence that response functions are usually convex, not S-shaped. Miles and Arnold, reviewing the literature, come to the same conclusion. Jones's STAS calculations,[3] and the AdTel study reported in Chapter 7, are further examples. So is the Bogart et al. print experiment discussed in Chapter 8, and the Time–Seagram study. It seems to be quite often the case that one exposure, or OTS, may serve as a sufficient stimulus for purchase "next time." Moreover, the S-shaped curve from the McDonald study, the most strongly quoted evidence on the other side, has been shown to be an artifact of one specific analysis, which looked at switches only averaged (or aggregated) across all brands in the market. If McDonald's results are analyzed on a share basis, they produce a similar pattern to the Jones STAS analyses.

Some papers, e.g., Rao and Miller, seem to contradict the evidence listed above by arguing that the response function is normally found to be S-shaped.[4] But what Rao and Miller are modeling is quite different: they are relating *aggregate* sales and advertising expenditure data and comparing districts that differed in expenditure rates. Districts in which advertising expenditure was relatively low produced lower incremental sales than districts where expenditure was moderate, and, at the other end, sales fall off when expenditure passes a certain point. All this has nothing directly to do with the frequency question, where we are concerned with what happens to individuals when they see more or less advertising before they purchase. It may well be explained in terms of competitive weights of expenditure: a critical Share of Voice level for a brand, both as floor and ceiling.

The basic problem we are immediately brought up against is that, as a conclusion, it is far too general. The common-sense view is that *sometimes* one is enough, at *other* times more are needed: the question is *when?* the most obvious factors being ignored are the status of the brand, the quality of the advertising, and the timing of the OTS.

Jones found that the brands with the most effective STAS tended to be the major players in the field—his so-called Alpha brands. The AdTel study suggests the same. These brands have attained a major share (largely as a result of continuing successful advertising and promotion), and now reap the benefit of the so-called "double jeopardy" effect: the larger the brand's market share, the less proportionately it has to spend on advertising to keep its position and beat the competition. This assumes, of course, that the brand continues to deliver perceived superior consumer benefits and that the advertising remains potent. Jones, AdTel, and McDonald all agree that *some* brands' advertising shows zero effectiveness, whatever the frequency: sometimes, these can be brands which in the past have had high shares and successful campaigns.

It seems logical that a large-share brand, whose main concern is to ensure repeat purchasing, and whose advertising is familiar and well-liked, should not require an overloaded frequency to keep the brand in view. When something has become familiar, the psychology of *learning* based on Ebbinghaus, which has been quoted to support the concept of a threshold, is not appropriate. Erwin Ephron argues convincingly that Krugman's three-exposure theory has been misused:

> Krugman's three stages, "What is it?", "What of it?" and, to paraphrase Krugman, "Oh, it's that damn commercial, again" describe the way people process information. We have *bent* his idea of *three psychological stages* into a rationale for *three message exposures.* The arrogance in our transformation is it tramples on Krugman's key point: "What is it?" and "What of it?" need happen *only once.* After the first two exposures, all subsequent exposures may be third exposures, reminders which simply serve to evoke the earlier messages.
>
> We are told "Krugman says" you need repetition to get people to learn and remember a message. If you read Krugman, here's what he says: "There is a myth in the advertising world that the viewer will forget your message if you don't repeat it often enough. . . . I would say the public comes closer to forgetting nothing they have seen on TV. . . . They just 'put it out of their minds' until and unless it has some use and (then) the response to the commercial continues".[5]

Thus, theoretically as well as in practice, there seems every reason to think that single exposures will work quite as well as multiple ones, *when what they are doing is reminding of something already familiar,* provided the spacing is controlled and the gaps not allowed to become too large. But that does not mean that the threshold idea is never appropriate. When might it be?

The obvious case is with a new message, especially if it is about a new brand. We know that new brands have to pay a high premium in terms of share of voice, to be noticed at all. The idea of a learning process, as well as the need for a sufficient presence to cut through the clutter, makes sense for a new introduction, which has to fight for a place against established competition. And not only new brands but also brands which are small-share or niche brands trying to widen their market. It is when looking at propensity to change, rather than reinforcement, that the McDonald data showed a slight tendency to an S-shaped curve.

If we follow Krugman, the threshold even in these cases may be temporary: once the message is learned or the brand grown, we may move into the repetition mode.

If the first 1979 conclusion no longer holds as a universal truth, neither will the second 1979 conclusion, which stated:

> Since one exposure is usually ineffective, the central goal of productive media planning should be to place emphasis on enhancing frequency rather than reach.

Again, it must depend on the situation: the status of the brand, its advertising history, the kind of competition it must expect to meet in its target market, and the timing implications of the purchase cycle, etc. It may, for example, be expected to apply to new products or innovations, but not to the established and familiar brand (see Conclusion 5). But, as a generalization, we would now prefer to abandon it.

Our second new conclusion repeats 1979's third with the addition of the word "probably" as follows:

> **Conclusion 2:** The weight of evidence suggests strongly that an exposure frequency of two within a purchase cycle is probably an effective level.

Whether we have a convex or a threshold response model, all the studies where we have a frequency measurement at all (i.e., probability of purchase following different frequencies) seem to suggest that two exposures are better than one and that attrition seems to start after two or, possibly, three. There is a possible exception for print advertising, where the Millward Brown evidence seems to suggest that wear-out can occur after the first exposure (or the first three OTS).[6]

However, many qualifications apply before we can interpret this statement. *Timing* is crucial: two exposures close together in time before a purchase occasion are a very different matter from two exposures several days or even weeks apart. *Share of voice* is crucial: two exposures for someone who is a heavy viewer, and sees many other advertisements for competing brands in the same period, is a very different matter from two exposures for a light viewer who sees relatively little competing advertising; one exposure in the latter case may be worth very much more to the advertiser than several exposures in the former. This principle applies whether we are talking about proven "exposures" or, as is more normal, OTS, where two OTS certainly means substantially less than two genuine exposures (another point we have to keep remembering). *Brand share, brand status,* and *advertising quality* are also all crucial.

It also should be noted that *some* of the evidence (e.g., Jones's STAS analyses[7] and some of the AdTel examples in Chapter 7) suggest that, even in television, the main effect occurs at 1 OTS and 2 or more add relatively little extra effect. There is not enough information to generalize under what conditions this occurs, or even whether some apparent differences are due to the data studied or the analysis design.

The 1979 edition followed with a fourth conclusion, that:

> By and large, optimal exposure frequency appears to be at least three exposures within a purchase cycle.

The evidence for this is less secure; the studies vary according to whether they show a sharp decrease in incremental effectiveness after two OTS or "exposures," or a continuation of the same rate of increase (it depends partly on exactly what is being measured). It seems to be true, for the most part, that three is an improvement over two, but this does not mean that it is necessarily a peak.

All the same caveats apply, especially that of timing. In the 1979 edition, a major advertiser was quoted, who had carried out an analysis of 38 brands over a four-week period. The criterion was unaided brand awareness. On the switching analysis theory, if the OTS or exposures had no effect, the proportion who became aware of the brand over the period (i.e., were aware of it at the end but not at the beginning) should equal those moving the other way (aware at the beginning but not at the end). It was found that those who received 0 or 1 exposures were negative (moved out of awareness); those receiving two were almost evenly balanced;

and it required three exposures to create a significantly positive effect. Above three exposures, the effect fluctuated at the same level, but did not increase. We are not told, however, whether all the brands were considered to have a four-week purchasing cycle, or what happened to brands that had their two, three, or more exposures distributed differently during the four weeks.

The truth is that there is no sound basis for generalization. We simply do not know how response will tend to vary over different time spans, for brands in different circumstances, with different criteria for measuring response. We have not done the necessary work to find out—it means studying a large number of actual cases. We are still thrown back almost wholly on "judgment" to decide on the "optimum" frequency level of an OTS within a defined period of time. Sometimes it may be three, but at least as often it may not.

We now therefore feel we must abandon any claim to an "optimal" exposure frequency within a purchase cycle. We replace it with a new conclusion that specifically addresses the issue of timing, as follows:

Conclusion 3: There is some quite good evidence that frequency, defined as a clustering of exposures or opportunities to see shortly before a purchase occasion, may increase the probability of a desired response, including in purchase probability.

Our fourth new conclusion considers the question of the convex curve, or diminishing returns:

Conclusion 4: There is good evidence that this effect tails off with larger frequencies above a certain level (a convex curve).

This now seems a more appropriate statement than the one made in 1979, which ran:

Beyond three exposures within a brand purchase cycle, or over a period of four or even eight weeks (as in the Ogilvy & Mather study), increasing frequency continues to build advertising effectiveness at a decreasing rate, but with no evidence of a decline.

It was said that this was noted in all the studies quoted in 1979.

The new evidence we have looked at in this edition, including the STAS findings, still seem to support this proposition, as far as television is concerned. If advertising works at all, it appears to go on working with repetition. The "decreasing rate" is attested by the apparent prevalence of the convex response function.

We need to be very careful here, however, of the confusion between the two senses of the term *frequency* that was pointed out in Chapter 8. Do we really mean frequency, occurring in a short time before the next purchase probability, or do we simply mean "repetition," which builds up over time interacting with purchasing patterns and experience of the brand? "Repetition" over a period may simply reinforce, and be best seen as a series of "frequencies of one." The diminishing but never quite level convex curve seems an entirely appropriate shape for the response to such repetition. It does not follow that it will apply to genuine "frequency." We know (from the McDonald study) that a frequency of two OTS in a short "window" of, say, four days before a purchase can increase the probability of buying; three or four OTS maintained it at this level, without increasing it still further. It seems very unlikely that an even higher concentration (e.g., 8 or 10,) would have done anything other than leave it at the same level still.

We must also note the evidence from Millward Brown, which indicates that print advertising behaves differently from television in this respect: whereas TV advertising, repeatedly viewed, appears able to increase advertising awareness (i.e., awareness that the brand has been advertised recently) indefinitely, print OTS above three (and therefore, perhaps, exposures after the first), add nothing to the same measure: instead of a slowly diminishing but still rising convex curve, you get a hump which rapidly declines from its peak. The conclusion needs a footnote: television behaves differently from print.

Our fifth new conclusion states:

Conclusion 5: There is no convincing evidence of a general rule which tells us what the optimum frequency should be. The biggest effect will often be at one exposure/OTS, especially if we are looking at large and familiar brands; in those cases, two, three, etc., will often add to one, but at lessening rate.

There are also cases where there is a "threshold," i.e., two or three exposures have more effect than one, tailing off thereafter; these are likely to be cases of newer or smaller brands seeking to establish rather than retain share, which must shout louder to be heard.

Our sixth new conclusion considers how the response curve may be affected by different factors:

Conclusion 6: The shape and steepness of the response curve, and whether or not there is a threshold, are affected by a large range of variables. These include:

- The brand's share and status.
- What the competition is doing.
- The quality of the advertising (bad advertising will not work whatever the frequency).
- The degree of clustering of the exposures on OTS.
- The timing of exposures/OTS in relation to the purchase cycle, their 'propinquity' to it (Wool).
- Share of voice, and whether the group being advertised to is a heavy or light consumer of media (because it may require more frequency/clustering to get a new message heard through a higher clutter of competing noise).
- Etc.

There is clear evidence that share of voice and proximity to the purchase occasion are both important in at least some cases. But, in general, not nearly enough results have been collected and studied, for different brands and campaigns to enable us to generalize about optimum frequencies and how they might vary.

Our remaining conclusions, 7 through 13, repeat the final seven from the 1979 edition; we have some comments to make, however, which may cast further light on some of them.

Conclusion 7: The frequency-of-exposure data from this review strongly suggest that wear-out is not a function of too much frequency per se. Indeed, wear-out is a copy or content problem.

Again, there seems to be a confusion here between the two senses of "frequency." We now have even more evidence (especially from the STAS results) that only good quality advertising works. Bad advertising will not even wear in. When advertising has the necessary quality, its continuing spread through the potential market follows "frequency-as-repetition"; as the campaign continues, more and more people have chances to see it and be reminded of it. This process is probably not affected at all by the fact that individuals may, from time to time, receive "frequency clusters" of OTS over short periods, which may influence their short-term purchase probabilities (but which, if overdone, may well exasperate the viewer).

We have not really proved that too much frequency per se, over short periods, may not be counterproductive. However, how enjoyable the advertising is must have a great deal to do with it. There has always been evidence of high quality campaign ideas which do not "wear-out," even over spans of several years, although the best of them refresh themselves from time to time with new executions.

Furthermore, we must note again the Millward Brown evidence (Conclusion 4) that print advertising does wear out even if television advertising does not, and that the success of print advertising (which can be considerable) therefore depends on the ability of a new execution to grip the attention of an interested reader the first time it is seen.

Conclusion 8: Very large and well-known brands—and/or those with dominant market shares in their categories and dominant shares of category advertising weight—appear to differ markedly from smaller or more average brands in response to frequency of exposure.

The evidence for this was drawn largely from the AdTel study (Chapter 7). It can be further endorsed, particularly following the STAS results. Large, successful and familiar brands have less work to do to remind consumers of their existence. Smaller and new brands have to work much harder to stand out against the clutter and be noticed. The general point about the advantages of a high brand share has been noted by several authorities.

Conclusion 9: Frequency of exposure has a differential effect on advertising response by daypart.

The evidence for this was the Ogilvy & Mather study (Chapter 6). It was said that the same finding should apply to print also, since recall scores vary by the thickness of the magazine.

We have nothing to add to this observation, first made in 1979. Clearly, the environment of OTS affects the likelihood that they will convert to exposures.

Conclusion 10: The greater the share of category exposures, the more positive the effects of frequency.

The McDonald study produced direct evidence of this. It is likely to be generally true, and may often be a better basis for analysis than the more numbers of OTS. But a high share will not outweigh a poor quality of advertising content.

Conclusion 11: Nothing we have seen suggests that frequency response principles or generalizations vary by medium.

In this edition we have looked at a number of print examples and found evidence of similar response to greater frequencies. But a very important caveat is that one is usually talking about delivery of exposure (or OTS) over very different time periods in relation to purchase cycles, usually taking much longer to build up in print.

In television advertising deliveries can be clustered in very short periods of time, but in print the insertion can only take place at the frequency of the issue and can only be repeated at no more than the same rate (at least within the same magazine). Moreover, we know from the Millward Brown work[8] that the actual buildup of OTS is much more gradual and spread out over time than the issue date (or publication intervals) would indicate. The implications for how one evaluates the frequency question are thus quite different. It is true, of course, that multiple insertions at the same time in different magazine titles that have a high duplicate readership *could* produce "frequency" clustering analogous to television, but this is likely to be relatively minor and hard to evaluate, given the above difficulties. At least with television, from metered audience data, one has a chance of knowing just when an OTS occurred in an individual household. The Millward Brown findings have made it impossible to know the same for an individual OTS in print.

We have to add to this the other Millward Brown suggestion that a print execution has virtually all its effect with just one exposure, and differs in this from television. Note the important point that this has only been established for one effectiveness measurement, advertising awareness. We have no knowledge whether it would work the same way for, e.g., purchase probabilities.

As a result, what we are dealing with in print is not "clustering," with greater or lesser extensions over time, so much as different "rates of repetition" at regular intervals. The evidence of Time–Seagram and other studies seems to point to convex (diminishing response) curves with slopes that vary inversely with the repetition rate: the shorter the interval between insertions, the steeper the slope.

Conclusion 12: Although there are general principles with respect to frequency of exposure and its relationship to advertising effectiveness, differential effects by brand are equally important.

Therefore, each brand should be examined to establish its own response function and how this varies in different circumstances, including good versus less good advertising.

We certainly still agree with this. It has been shown by Jones's STAS results and was also in evidence in the McDonald study.

Conclusion 13: The leverage of different equal-expenditure media plans in terms of frequency response can be substantial.

This was shown clearly in the AdTel study, where two different media plans were studied in respect of two of the brands. We have nothing to add to this, and no reason to disagree with it.

SUMMARY OF REVISED CONCLUSIONS

Conclusion 1: There is convincing evidence that advertising, when it is good enough to work at all, may have short-term effects, including effects of purchase probability.

Conclusion 2: The weight of evidence suggests strongly that an exposure frequency of two within a purchase cycle is probably an effective level.

Conclusion 3: There is some quite good evidence that frequency, defined as a clustering of exposures or opportunities to see shortly before a purchase occasion, may increase the probability of a desired response, including in purchase probability.

Conclusion 4: There is good evidence that this effect tails off with larger frequencies above a certain level (a convex curve).

Conclusion 5: There is no convincing evidence of a general rule that tells us what the optimum frequency should be. The major effect will often be at one exposure/OTS, especially if we are looking at large and familiar brands. In those cases, two, three, etc., will often add to one, but at lessening rate.

There are also cases where there is a "threshold," i.e., two or three exposures have more effect than one, tailing off thereafter. These are likely to be cases of newer or smaller brands seeking to establish rather than retain share, which must shout louder to be heard.

Conclusion 6: The shape and steepness of the response curve, and whether or not there is a threshold, are affected by a large range of variables. These include:

- The brand's share and status.

- What the competition is doing.

- The quality of the advertising (bad advertising will not work whatever the frequency).

- The degree of clustering of the exposures or OTS.

- The timing of exposures/OTS in relation to the purchase cycle, their "propinquity" to it.

- Share of voice, and whether the group being advertised to is a heavy or light consumer of media (because it may require more frequency/clustering to get a new message heard through a higher clutter of competing noise).

- Etc.

Conclusion 7: The frequency-of-exposure data from this review strongly suggests that wearout is not a function of too much frequency per se. Indeed, wearout is a copy or content problem.

Conclusion 8: Very large and well-known brands—and/or those with dominant market shares in their categories and dominant shares of category advertising weight—appear to differ markedly in response to frequency of exposure from smaller or more average brands.

Conclusion 9: Frequency of exposure has a differential effect on advertising response by daypart.

Conclusion 10: The greater the share of category exposures, the more positive the effects of frequency.

Conclusion 11: Nothing we have seen suggests that frequency response principles or generalizations vary by medium.

Conclusion 12: Although there are general principles with respect to frequency of exposure and its relationship to advertising effectiveness, differential effects by brand are equally important.

Conclusion 13: The leverage of different equal-expenditure media plans in terms of frequency response can be substantial.

WHAT STILL NEEDS TO BE FOUND OUT

These new conclusions are still uncomfortably vague. There is some generality about them, but it would be dangerous to take them, uncritically, at face value as rules for any particular brand. We are still almost totally dependent on "judgment" in respect of the campaign we happen at any time to be interested in.

To get beyond that judgment, there is no substitute for studying the individual brand and its category, so as to understand how its purchasers buy it and how, in doing so, they interact with the exposures or OTS they actually receive over time. It is necessary to know what the purchase cycles are and how they vary, and how OTS deliveries vary for those with different patterns of consumption (light or heavy viewers, readers or nonreaders, etc.).

In principle, for many product categories, the raw material for such pragmatic study is at hand, with single-source data. This should provide the means to interlace, for the same individual consumers over long periods of time, patterns of OTS with patterns of purchasing. We know that the analysis is possible; what is needed is the gathering of widespread, practical, *knowledge* of different examples. It must be a major disappointment that the promise of this kind of data source, eagerly looked forward to in the 1979 edition, still remains largely unfulfilled (with the exception of the new Nielsen data from which the STAS calculations are being made). There have, it is true, been serious problems, notably the difficulty of recording transmitted commercials in a multi-channel environment. But technology exists to cope with such problems, if the need is recognized and the investment is forthcoming. The best hope for progress in the understanding for which we continually strain must be that advertisers perceive the need to fund, and pursue, from single-source and other available data, *detailed* understanding of how the buying process works for their own brands.

It is an easy matter to list analyses which it would be desirable to do across brands, so as to refine the generalizations we are able to make, supposing that funds could be made available for a combined and publishable effort. The problem always comes down to there being so many *sources of variation* that, combined, seem to make each case unique. The analyses that need to be done, from the data sources available, are those that would enable us to better evaluate these variations. Here is a candidate list that could easily be added to:

1. From single-source data. Using STAS and similar analysis methods, find out how the brand purchase response function varies against 0, 1, 2, 3, 4, etc., OTS, in the following different circumstances:

    - When the OTS are clustered v. spread out over time.

    - When the most recent OTS occur 1, 2, 4, 7, etc., days before purchase.

    - When there is also exposure to various types of promotion, or none.

    - According to different patterns of category and brand purchase.

    - In different contexts of exposure to OTS for competitors. In particular, when does frequency appear to be necessary to "cut through" competition and when does it not.

    - For different creative contexts, especially comparing executions that are known to have been successes or failures.

    - Between different media, or media combinations.

    - For brands with different share levels (leaders and also-rans), and between established brands and newcomers.

- Between old and new executions for established brands.

It ought to be possible to gather together analyses of existing single-source data to pull out comparisons on these levels, plus at least some of the possible interactions between them:

2. From tracking and attitude data. Where single-source is not available or suitable, it should still be possible to study responses to advertising, even if the connections are less direct, making many of the comparisons listed above. Different criterion measures should be compared for the response effects they are able to show, and evaluated:

- Sales (EPOS) data

- IRI-type test marketing

- Advertising awareness measures (i.e., awareness that the brand has been advertised recently)

- Advertising recognition measures (playback of specific executions)

- Communication measures

- Brand awareness measures

It would be a major cooperative task, requiring agreement from advertisers and others on a wide scale, to gather together the necessary data and submit it to these analyses. Only a candidate list, there would undoubtedly be more ideas than are suggested here. But in principle it could be done, without collecting much if any new data, if enough were willing to take part. The purpose would be to try, gradually, to impose a clearer outline on the somewhat vague and misty picture which still remains when we look at response functions, however defined: not by removing or averaging out the variations which exist, but by identifying better when they occur, so that in particular cases they can be expected and allowed for.

NOTES

1. Julian L. Simon and Johan Arndt, "The Shape of the Advertising Response Function," *Journal of Advertising Research,* vol. 20, no. 4 (August 1980): 11–28. Morgan

P. Miles and Danny R. Arnold, "What Marketers Know about the Effective Frequency Construct," *Journal of Media Planning* (Spring 1990): 42–56. John P. Jones, *When Ads Work: New Proof That Advertising Triggers Sales* (New York: Lexington Books, 1995).

2. Simon and Arndt, "The Shape of the Advertising Response Function."

3. Jones, *When Ads Work.*

4. Ambar G. Rao and Peter B. Miller, "Advertising/Sales Response Functions," *Journal of Advertising Research,* vol. 15, no. 2 (April 1975): 7–15.

5. Erwin Ephron, "The Trouble with Flighting." Draft of a presentation to the A.N.A. Television Forum, February 8, 1994.

6. Gordon Pincott, "An Examination of Wear-out and Exposure over Time," Millward Brown International, June 1993. See also Gordon Brown, "Attention and Memory for TV and Magazines," *Admap* (January 1994): 15–20.

7. Jones, *When Ads Work.*

8. Ephron, "The Trouble with Flighting." See also Pincott, "An Examination of Wearout."

CHAPTER 10

IMPLICATIONS FOR MEDIA PLANNING

The 1979 edition of this book was published against the background of increasing interest in the idea of "effective frequency" as a basis for media planning, not least because, as explained in our first chapter, it seemed to offer more cost-effectiveness and less waste. The concept was further boosted, not merely by the book and the debates that followed, but by the increasing availability of technology that could do the necessary calculations:

The availability, through such firms as Telmar and IMS, of large-scale data bases and the powerful capabilities of time-sharing computer analyses offered by such firms have placed reach and frequency distribution models at the fingertips of media planners and buyers. The widespread use of such models has also been encouraged by industry-wide studies such as that of the ANA study on "effective reach applications.[1]

And Turk, following his opinion survey among senior media executives, concluded:

Effective frequency planning has achieved an integral role in the media planning of the largest consumer product agencies in the United States.[2]

CRITICISMS

At the same time, the effective frequency concept was, and continues to be, subjected to critical questioning. Much of the criticism has already been discussed in earlier chapters. We can summarize the various lines of criticism as follows:

1. *Lack of empirical evidence.*
   Many practitioners accept his (Naples's) guidelines for effective media planning as true without the benefit of empirical support. . . .

   The subsequent analysis (of 20 studies listed) reveals that there is very little agreement on the impact of frequency on attitude toward brand or purchasing behavior. Naples' (1979) capstone assessment of effective frequency leaves many pragmatic issues unresolved. The most crucial conceptual gaps facing practitioners pertain to how the effect of advertising on consumer behavior should be measured and what the optimal number of exposures required to achieve a given communication objective are. The utilization of single source integrated metered data bases in empirical studies should help resolve this issue.[3]

   • • •

   The degree of utilization is somewhat surprising in light of the relatively limited experience agencies have had with message distribution data. It seemed logical to expect the development would be slower until reliable field research data could be correlated with frequency strategies.[4]

2. *Recognition of other variables that affect the issue.*
   Different commentators have recognized the crucial importance of *timing,*[5] also called "spacing,"[6] *propinquity,* or timing in relation to the purchase,[7] *competition* and *share of voice factors.*[8] All of these can effect whether, and how, frequency might "work" at different levels. Another source of variation is the criterion taken for "effectiveness," whether awareness, attitude, or purchase probability.

3. *The relevance of psychological learning theory.*
   The relevance of psychological learning theory in the versions attributed to Ebbinghaus, Krugman, etc., have been questioned, e.g., by Priemer and Ephron.[9] It may be applicable to some advertising, involving the absorption of new messages, but does not seem appropriate to advertising that simply recalls to mind what is already

familiar. It ignores the ability of human beings to remember over very long periods things that happen to interest them, as well as to screen out instantly the much larger number of things that do not. "Media planners have not fully addressed the issue of consumer involvement. . . . Petty, Cacioppo and Schumann (1985) suggest that consumer involvement with the product may be a crucial factor in the outcome of increased levels of frequency."[10] Krugman's "What is it?—What of it?" progression may apply the first time a new campaign is seen, but the third and subsequent exposures simply remind: it follows that, if a reminder ad may act as a trigger, any one such reminder may be enough to serve, provided the recipient is "in the market" at the time."[11]

This question links with the shape of the response function. There has been much evidence quoted (e.g., Simon and Arndt, Miles and Arnold, Jones) that the commonest shape is the convex curve, which opens the possibility that a single exposure or OTS can be effective in at least a number of common marketing situations, even if two or three are more so. All of this throws doubt on any suggestion that there is a *standard* optimum frequency level, such as three, which should always be aimed for.[12]

4. *The OTS/exposure dilemma.*
Many commentators (e.g., Sissors, Cannon and Goldring)[13] have taken up the point that what most media calculations deliver is OTS, not proven exposures. Thus, if 2 OTS are better than 1, it may simply mean that those receiving 2 OTS have more chance of having 1 exposure. This probably does not matter very much, so long as the empirical measures are also in OTS. Unlike exposures, OTS are a convenient and observable currency. The danger comes only when we mix the two up in the same argument, so it is important to keep aware of the distinction.

5. *Media factors.*
There are also questions about different media vehicles. Achenbaum, for example, believes[14] that effective frequency should only apply to television: since no one ever reads anything in a magazine more than once, reach is what is important for print; the relationship between "exposures" and OTS is very different for TV and print (TV "loses" much more than print does). The non-comparability of what is delivered by OTS in different media is, of course, a long-standing problem in media planning, so that this question is not a

new one. Carat's "Memorization" models in Europe[15] are one attempt to give a common meaning to reach and frequency value estimates between, and combining, different media.

USE OF THE "EFFECTIVE FREQUENCY" CONCEPT

Despite these uncertainties, and many others (including worries about the quality of the research data on which the estimating procedures are based, as well as of the models themselves), media planning still, as a rule, involves making some judgment about an appropriate level of frequency for a particular campaign. Although this is not a book about how to do media planning (it would have to be at least twice the size), it seems right to conclude with a brief look, in principle, at how the concept fits in when it is used.

The first practical problem is that the "average frequency" estimates delivered by scheduling programs are strictly meaningless abstracts. They merely summarize a wide distribution, few of whose values are in fact close to the "average." Thus, if we specified "an average frequency per week of 3 OTS," the schedule would only deliver 3 OTS in a minority of cases. This is well illustrated by the example in Table 10.1 (a genuine analysis of BARB data), quoted in an article by Gullen and Hulks, then of JWT, in 1982.[16]

EFFECTIVE REACH

Both schedules deliver about 5 OTS on average, but less than 10 percent are actually at 5, and the range from 0 to 11+ is very wide. One way of simplifying such a frequency distribution is to divide the recipients into equally sized groups, e.g., tertiles or quintiles (the authors call this "a particularly North American way of evaluating the distribution of opportunities to see"). Another way, however, which has become more common is the notion of "effective reach": to single out the range of frequencies which we consider most valuable, and design the schedule to maximize the proportion falling into that range. It can easily be seen that "effective reach" is thus the practical expression of the theory of "effective frequency"; its application to the real-life frequency distribution. We could decide, for example, that the effective reach would be any frequency

Table 10.1 Frequency Analysis

	Schedule 1	Schedule 2
All h/w	(217)	(217)
Total TVR	400	397
1+ cover	82%	84%
Average OTS	4.9	4.7
H/w with children	(71)	(71)
Total TVR	375	461
1+ cover	83%	89%
Average OTS	4.5	5.2
H/w with children:		
no. of spots seen	%	%
None	18.4	16.1
1	14.3	11.1
2	12.4	14.8
3	7.8	10.0
4	11.1	11.1
5	4.2	8.8
6	8.0	7.8
7	10.0	5.1
8	4.2	5.1
9	2.3	3.2
10	3.2	1.8
11+	6.6	5.5

between two and six, or two and ten, or even one and some higher number, depending on the product and the audience. In the example in Table 10.1, if effective reach is defined as the proportion seeing between two and eight spots, it was calculated to have the following values:

	Schedule 1	Schedule 2
All h/w		
Total TVR	400	397
Net cover	82%	84%
Effective reach	58%	65%
H/w with children		
Total TVR	375	461
Net cover	83%	89%
Effective reach	63%	72%

This shows clearly that Schedule 2 was better at reaching housewives with children, assuming that the 2–8 OTS range is correctly chosen as being most "effective."

The concept of "effective reach" is not new. Alvin Achenbaum in a paper in 1977,[17] quoted in Chapters 1 and 6 of the 1979 edition, introduced a concept of "effective rating points," also based on the idea of trying to maximize the proportion who receive the range of frequencies judged to be effective. He explained in a later paper in 1986 that he intended this term to comprise three elements: frequency, reach and continuity, so that it would replace "gross rating points" and apply across all media boundaries.[18]

However, awareness of a concept does not imply its use. Leckenby and Kishi, in their 1982 survey of media planning practice,[19] found that "frequency distribution and, particularly, effective reach were not used as frequently as more conventional standards of schedule evaluation such as reach, GRPs, average frequency, and CPM to target market." Doubts about both the models available and the underlying research base were adduced as explanations; one respondent said that effective reach "like effective frequency . . . needs to be "glamorized" and then it will be accepted." Craig and Ghosh also refer to the shortcomings of available models: "One of the reasons for this disparity, between heavy reliance on total reach and the generally acknowledged merits of effective reach, is the difficulty of using the latter as an evaluative criterion in presently available media scheduling algorithms."[20]

However, some scheduling programs employing effective reach and integrating different media have been described, e.g., at J. Walter Thompson.[21] Craig and Ghosh, in a later paper, say that "extensive efforts have been undertaken to develop mathematical models . . . aided by the rapid advances in computer technology and quality of data available, these models have increased in their sophistication and utility."[22]

It is clear that many of these developed models, including those Craig and Ghosh illustrate in their paper, have assumed the "three-hit rule," following Krugman as he has been understood. Murray and Jenkins,[23] in a review of the "effective reach" concept, conclude that the best assumptions to make are as follows:

1. Three confirmed vehicle exposures to an individual or household in the target audience over a prescribed time period provide a realistic, pragmatic definition of "effective reach."

2. As a general rule, a "reach threshold" of 45 percent of the target audience over an agreed-upon time period is an appropriate minimum level of effective reach.

3. In television "a one-week reach of 45 to 50 percent, interestingly, is also likely to achieve a four-week effective reach of 45 to 50 percent." The authors expect that other research in progress will show equivalent results for other media.

4. The minimum requirement for effective reach in outdoor media is twelve or more vehicle exposures per month.

5. The minimum requirement for effective reach for radio, television, and newspapers is three or more vehicle exposures per month.

6. The minimum requirement for effective reach in magazines is three or more vehicle exposures per quarter.

Murray and Jenkins claim to have reached these conclusions as a result of "an analysis of hundreds of media schedules, conducted in Canada over the past three decades." In particular, the second conclusion, that 45 percent is the appropriate minimum level for effective reach, is "based on the authors' empirical market experience with a wide variety of goods and services." They "have experimented with several different levels of reach and frequency, using different media." In these experiments, those achieving effective reach of 45 percent or more of the designated target audience over a designated time period "resulted in marketplace success on almost all occasions" (marketplace success being defined as "performance that equals or surpasses the previously defined market objectives of the advertiser)". But when reach fell below 45 percent, "relatively few marketplace successes resulted." The exceptions in both cases could be explained by special circumstances.

This account of the analysis of several campaigns over the years is mouth-watering stuff. It underscores our belief that the only way to make progress in this field is to look at real data and case histories on just such a wide scale. We would like to know more detail. Murray and Jenkins are tantalizing in what they do not tell us, especially their justification for setting three exposures over "an agreed-upon time period" as the criterion for effective reach. It is not clear from the paper whether they have independent evidence for the "three-hit theory," or are simply accepting Krugman.

PERSUASION VERSUS REMINDING

Elliott, quoting the McDonald evidence on the difference between "retentive" effects (the REPEAT measure) and "attractive" effects (the CHANGE measure), distinguishes two main advertising strategies that affect frequency:

1. *A "maintenance" strategy.* When advertising's role is to reinforce imagery, maintain the purchase habit, retain purchasers; *and* when competitive activity is light; then 1 or 2 OTS per product purchase interval is optimum. In practice, to aim for a frequency of 1 OTS per interval, but covering twice as many intervals, may well be the more cost-effective route.

2. *A "change" or competitive strategy.* When advertising's role is to modify attitudes, alter behavior, gain switches; *or* when competition is heavy; then 2+ OTS per purchase interval is better.

These may look like low levels of frequency. They are not. It takes a very large budget, or a very infrequent purchase cycle, to cover even most of the year at these OTS levels. How many brands, for instance, can afford a TV exposure level as high as one OTS per fortnight?[24]

This quotation illustrates the importance for the budget, if nothing else, of making the right judgment about the effective frequency level appropriate to one's case. It depends not only on all the other variables we have been discussing, but also on one's *marketing objective*—what one is trying to do. A wasteful level is expensive as well as unproductive.

It follows (generally) that a "maintenance" strategy as described here may be more likely to be best served by continuous advertising, to deliver the 1 or 2 frequency level, whereas a "change" strategy will tend to occur in bursts, if only because that is all that can be afforded. Elliott also comments, as have many others, that "threshold" levels of effectiveness have increased over the years. With more clutter and more media alternatives, one may have to shout louder to be heard, even in a high-frequency burst.

FREQUENCY AND COMPETITIVE NOISE

This brings us to an argument that is often advanced in favor of setting high frequency levels such as the "3+ rule": you need it in order to "cut through" the competing noise. With new advertising, the learning theory says that more than one exposure is needed to take the message on board; even with reminder advertising, from another point of view, several OTS may be needed to ensure that sufficient people have the chance of even one exposure.

A number of commentators[25] point out that this presupposes a somewhat passive view of the consumer of advertising. On the contrary, people respond to what happens to interest them at the time and/or is attractive in itself: thus, good creative advertising only needs one viewing to draw the relevant consumers, however buried in clutter, whereas twenty poor advertisements will fail to be noticed. Unfortunately, however true this is, it may not be all that much help to the media planner, who does not usually know at the time of planning how creatively effective the ad is going to be, and might be unwise to assume the best.

In making the right judgments about how to deal with clutter and competitive noise, a number of aspects suggest themselves for consideration:

1. How good is the competition? We know from the McDonald evidence, and from Jones's Nielsen data, that good competitive campaigns can "win" over inferior ones. A higher frequency may be needed to confront a very effective competitor campaign. Alternatively, if that is too expensive, we may wish to avoid direct confrontation. It may depend on how confident we are in the creative ability of our campaign to be noticed.

2. Timing and placing. One of the problems with television is that even heavy viewers have days or even weeks when they see little or no TV. Thus, their viewing of all commercials, our competitors' as well as our own, tends to be concentrated into the same time spans; if they receive a high frequency of our advertising at any one time, they will also receive high frequencies of other people's advertising during the same times. This is clearly evident from studies of panel data, including both McDonald and Jones. It intensifies the "competitive noise" problem. Ephron suggests that the more a planner

goes for frequency on television, the less effective he will progressively be, because the extra GRPs will fall increasingly into the "black hole" of the heavy viewers' viewing times, when they already have more than enough opportunities to see.[26]

There may be a case (depending on the brand's situation and style of advertising, etc.) for contrary thinking: spreading one's effort over the lighter viewers, or into print, away from where the competitive noise is, so that a lower frequency may be more "effective." "Effective frequency" (at least in the shape of the "3+ rule") has been seen as a rationale for flighting, because that is the only way it can be afforded. But if we interpret it in a more open-minded way (e.g., that effectiveness for some campaigns may mean a frequency of one), this connection disappears.

What we know about "effective frequency" does nothing to resolve the question of whether flighting is or is not a better strategy than continuous advertising, or the related questions of whether a concentrated frequency with a low reach is usually "better" than a lower frequency with a higher reach. This has to be decided on other grounds; ideally, with more knowledge from single-source data and the like, which we still lack, about how brands of the type we are concerned with actually respond.

3. The purchasing cycle. There is clear evidence (McDonald, Jones) that timing in relation to the purchase cycle is important: an exposure closely before a purchase, at least for regularly bought products, is likely to be worth more than two exposures some time before. Again, we still know far too little about just how this works, e.g., how response to stimuli build up as one approaches closer to the purchase, how it varies with (e.g.) new campaigns as opposed to reminders, etc.

Media planners, obviously, cannot work directly with purchase cycles, since these are unpredictable at the individual level. Schedules have to be in terms of calendar days or weeks (customarily, four weeks). But for many product categories we know (or could know, from panel data) several general points about the purchase cycle: its average length, the distribution around that average, and the days of the week on which purchases usually are made by the target group. Arranging for spots to coincide with these timings, such as the day or two before the day on which shopping trips tend to take place, should be child's play to a media planner.

This applies obviously to television and radio. But it is relevant to print also. We have the capacity to know, or learn, when print media tend to be read, how potential OTS build up for target groups who duplicate their magazine reading, and the timings at which insertions in a particular issue deliver the full complement of OTS. (The Millward Brown study has shown that this takes a long time, much longer than the "four-week schedule."[27]

MULTIPLICATION OF MODELS

The fragmentation of television is gradually making the attainment of simple "reach" a harder option to achieve. At the same time, there is an explosive increase in available (and affordable) software, which makes the calculation and modeling of frequency distributions progressively easier to do. These trends, working together, are making effective frequency a hotter issue in media planning.

It is now possible to use the computer to "try out" a whole range of frequency assumptions and see which best fit the evidence. A recent example, described by Gullen and Copage at a conference in November 1993,[28] is the CRAM system (short for Carat Research Awareness Model). This takes a schedule (e.g., television rating points, from BARB data), and calculates what it would have been expected to achieve on various assumptions about effective frequency, e.g., whether the effective trigger for awareness is 1+, 2+, etc. A very large number of such models ("typically 50 or so") are produced. The trick then is to compare them with actual tracking data for, say, advertising awareness (which seems to be the commonest, though not the only, measure used), and see which model or models fits the results best: this is then taken to be the optimum frequency for the brand. Sometimes it is found that several different frequency assumptions fit the data almost equally well, and in such cases it is concluded that frequency is an inappropriate target: 1+ is as likely to be effective as 5+.

Since this is a proprietary system, Carat Research naturally does not say too much about it, and several of the questions we have already been looking at come to mind: do the models take account of time spread and clustering of OTS? What is meant exactly by 2+ cover? And can they compare between different media, when, as we have seen, response curves in print may follow a very different trajectory from television? The

CRAM system is not singled out here for approval (we are in no position to pass judgment on it), but simply as an illustration of the kind of endeavor now going on in media planning agencies. They are aware that a good proprietary system for dealing with the effective frequency question is a worthwhile prize, and many of them are making considerable efforts to develop their own approach.

The trouble is that the models which computers produce so effortlessly can look very like attempts to spin straw into gold, unless they can be anchored to real research evidence, of which, as we have argued previously, there is still not nearly enough. Knowing what has actually happened in previous campaigns with the brand in question may well be as close as we can get, although there is still a large assumption involved (that the future will be the same as the past).

CONCLUDING COMMENTS

This brief review can only give a faint outline of the art of media planning. As we said earlier, this is not a book about media planning. What it illustrates boils down to one basic point. The "effective frequency" concept—that there is a range of frequencies which is more useful than others, depending on the campaign—is an important part of the planner's agenda: it suggests a check list of things he must look out for. What it is *not* is a "rule," least of all a simplistic rule of the form "three plus is optimal." The real world is too complex and variable for such a rule to work:

> The danger is that for almost any general question on almost any subject there exists a very simple, straightforward, easy to understand and most *wrong* answer. So it is with Effective Frequency.[29]

It has been argued that, in so far a planners have adopted the "3+ rule," they may well have set back their art and caused considerable budgetary waste in the process.[30] It was not the intention of our 1979 edition to lead to that, nor is it now.

As an agenda-setting concept rather than a "rule," "effective frequency" has a clear value. It forces people to think through what could happen under various assumptions about media delivery, and from there what they want to happen and how to come closest to achieving it. It also helps to underline for us the continuing limits of our knowledge. Virtually all the studies covered in this book have been of an experimental nature, claiming only to study a part of the problem, and not safe to generalize from; at each point in the argument, we have found ourselves identifying areas where we would like to know more. This is bound to be the case, from the very nature of the subject. There is no universal knowledge possible in the real, ever-changing consumers' world. Knowledge is gained in this setting, not by single blockbusting experiments, but by painstaking gathering and recording of information from different examples—natural history, not fundamental physics.

There is no cause for despair, once this is realized. We have learned progressively more over the years about natural history and about consumer behavior. The capacity to find out how consumers respond to advertising campaigns in particular has grown considerably over the past decade, not least in the still woefully underused resource—single-source panel data. We could, with the data sources we now have, do much to illuminate the uncertainties, simply by showing what happened in similar cases. The best guidance for what to do with our brand, now, is a range of evidence about what has succeeded or failed with similar brands in the past, under different conditions of cluster, repetition, competitive clutter, timing, and so on. The data deposits are present and growing all the time; they are not yet being effectively mined.

The point has been well put by Phil Gullen, then responsible for media planning effectiveness at JWT London, now Managing Director of Carat Research in the UK:

> To fulfill clients' needs in the future, media departments and independents must try to understand the complexities of the new environment. To do this in the most meaningful way they need to move away from media efficiency as the *sole* criterion of success, and towards a much greater focus on effectiveness. This is what I call upgrading to *high definition media planning.*
>
> High definition media planning uses targets focused on effectiveness such as a sales response from advertising, or changes in attitude. By comparison, low definition media planning uses targets defined as simple media scores such as ratings, conversion factors, CPT, etc.
>
> To maximize effectiveness, a media planner needs to put himself in the shoes of the consumers, and ask how they will see the campaign. Who are they? How many ads will they see? In which media? Over what period of time? In what context? All of these things are the key to effectiveness, keys to moving into high definition media planning.[31]

NOTES

1. J. D. Leckenby and S. Kishi, "How Media Directors View Reach/Frequency Estimation," *Journal of Advertising Research,* vol. 22, no. 3 (June/July 1982): 64–69.

2. Peter B. Turk, "Effective Frequency Report: Its Use and Evaluation by Major Agency Media Department Executives," *Journal of Advertising Research* (April/May 1988): 55–59.

3. M. P. Miles and D. R. Arnold, "What Marketers Know About the Effective Frequency Construct," *Journal of Media Planning* (Spring 1990): 42–56.

4. Turk, "Effective Frequency Report."

5. E. Papazian, "Mediology," *Marketing and Media Decisions* (June 1986): 85–86.

6. August B. Priemer, "New Alternatives to Effective Frequency in Media Planning," *Journal of Media Planning* (Fall 1986): 25–28.

7. Abbott Wool, "Elements of Media: Frequency vs. Propinquity," *Mediaweek* (July 26, 1993): 19. Erwin Ephron, "The Trouble with Flighting." Draft presentation intended to be made to the ANA Television Forum, February 8, 1994.

8. Jack Z. Sissors, "Confusions About Effective Frequency: Semantics and Measurement Problems," *Journal of Advertising Research,* vol. 22, no. 6 (December 1982/January 1983): 33–37. Also "Advice to Media Planners on How to Use Effective Frequency," *Journal of Media Planning* (Fall 1986): 3–9. M. K. Ray and P. H. Webb, "Three Prescriptions for Clutter," *Journal of Advertising Research* (February/March 1986): 69–77.

9. Priemer, "New Alternatives," and Erwin Ephron, "The Rule of Three?" *Inside Media* (January 8, 1992).

10. Miles and Arnold, "What Marketers Know."

11. L. Bogart, B. S. Tolley, and F. Orenstein, "What One Little Ad Can Do," *Journal of Advertising Research,* vol. 10, no. 4 (August 1970): 3–13.

12. Julian L. Simon and Johan Arndt, "The Shape of the Advertising Response Function," *Journal of Advertising Research,* vol. 20, no. 4 (August 1980): 11–28. John Philip Jones, *When Ads Work: New Proof That Advertising Triggers Sales* (New York, Lexington Books, 1995).

13. Sissors, "Confusion About Effective Frequency." H. Cannon and N. Goldring, "Another Look at Effective Frequency," *Journal of Media Planning* (Fall 1986): 29–36.

14. Alvin A. Achenbaum, "Effective Exposure: The Subversion of a Useful Idea," *Journal of Media Planning* (Fall 1986): 11–12.

15. Alan Copage, "Life Without Television," *Admap* (October 1993): 24–27.

16. P. Gullen and R. Hulks, "Beyond Cost per Thousand in Television," *Admap* (October 1983): 494–502.

17. Alvin A. Achenbaum, "Effective Exposure: A New Way of Evaluating Media." Address to the 1977 A.N.A. Media Workshop, New York, February 3, 1977.

18. Achenbaum, "Effective Exposure: The Subversion of a Useful Idea."

19. Leckenby and Kishi, "How Media Directors View Reach/Frequency Estimation."

20. Samuel C. Craig and Avijit Ghosh, "Maximizing Effective Reach in Media Planning." Paper delivered at the American Marketing Association Education Conference, Summer 1985.

21. Gullen and Hawks, "Beyond Cost per Thousand in Television." P. Gullen, "Planning Media to Create Sales," *Admap* (October 1985): 505–11. P. Gullen, "High Definition Media Planning: How Media Planning and Research Must Adapt," *Admap* (December 1991): 30–34.

22. Samuel C. Craig and Avijit Ghosh, "Using Household-level Viewing Data to Maximize Effective Reach," *Journal of Advertising Research* (January/February 1993): 38–47.

23. George G. Murray and John R. G. Jenkins, "The Concept of Effective Reach in Advertising," *Journal of Advertising Research* (May/June 1992): 34–42.

24. Jeremy Elliott, "How Advertising Frequency Affects Advertising Effectiveness: Indications of Change," *Admap* (October 1985): 512–15.

25. H. Cannon, "A Theory-based Approach to Optimal Frequency," *Journal of Media Planning* (Fall 1986): 33–44. Sissors, "Confusions about Effective Frequency."

26. Erwin Ephron, "A New Network Reach Strategy." Draft article, 1993.

27. Gullen, "High Definition Media Planning."

28. Phil Gullen and Alan Copage, "Effective Frequency—Are We Chasing Rainbows?" Paper delivered at Media Research Group Conference, Amsterdam, November 1993.

29. R. Warrens, "Seeing What the Viewer Sees," *Journal of Media Planning* (Fall 1986): 51–52.

30. Jones, "When Ads Work."

31. Gullen, "High Definition Media Planning."

INDEX

147

ABOUT THE AUTHORS

Colin McDonald is a leading media researcher and analyst. He was responsible for the world's first single-source analysis, which proved that short-term advertising effects on purchasing could be measured. He is president of his own UK-based consultancy, McDonald Research, which specializes in the design, conduct, and interpretation of media and advertising research.

Michael J. Naples, author of the first edition, is President of the Advertising Research Foundation. Previously, he was Director of Marketing Research for Lever Brothers Company.